C STRUIK (PTY) LTD
56 WALE STREET
CAPE TOWN

THIRD
IMPRESSION
1977

COPYRIGHT
© 1975
GERALD CUBITT
AND
ARNOLD HELFET

ISBN 0 86977 102 7

ART DIRECTION AND DESIGN
BY WILLEM JORDAAN, CAPE TOWN
LITHOGRAPHIC REPRODUCTIONS
BY HIRT & CARTER (PTY) LTD, CAPE TOWN
PHOTOSET BY
McMANUS BROS (PTY) LTD, CAPE TOWN
PRINTED AND BOUND BY
CREDA PRESS (PTY) LTD,
CAPE TOWN

Contents

4 | Publisher's Note
6 | Introduction
7 | South Africa
33 | Cape Province
109 | Natal
143 | Orange Free State
155 | Transvaal
206 | Map of South Africa
208 | List of Sources

Introduction

Everything about the land-mass that is Africa is big, impressive, unique and, intriguingly, in many ways still mysteriously unknown.

This vast continent stretches 8 000 km southward from Tangier to Cape Town, separated from Europe by only 14 km of water, where the mouth of the Mediterranean is guarded by the Rock of Gibraltar.

Novelists of yore wrote romantically about Darkest Africa. More recently it became the Awakening Giant. Today it is a news-gathering conglomeration made up of countless nationalities, tribes, ethnic groups and religious entities.

Likewise, this enormous land is the stamping ground of the greatest variety of animal and bird life in the world, and its geographic and geophysical make-up are as interesting and varied as is its profusion of flora, from the exotic to the rare to the unusual.

Africa, all 28 830 000 km² of it, is like no other continent comprising as it does no less than 48 countries, which represent approximately 36% of the entire United Nations membership. Yet the Republic of South Africa is large even in its African context. It covers the enormous southern end, a chunk of 1 280 000 km² and is in turn vastly different to the diverse others to her north. To begin with it has far more White citizens than all the rest of the continent. Whereas South Africa subsisted mainly on an agricultural economy until 100 years ago, she is today the most industrialised and possibly the richest and most powerful country in Africa. An interesting comparison in this regard is that South Africa produces and consumes more steel and electricity than all the 47 other African countries together. It is common knowledge that gold forms the backbone of the Republic's economy. That gold is indeed her largest single currency earner is borne out by the fact that she produces 77% of this mineral in the Free World. However, in addition, almost all minerals and basic raw materials, with the exception of oil, are to be found in South Africa. Strong indications are that oil will be found sooner or later. For the present she is fortunate indeed that only 15% of her energy requirements depend on imported oil. Her mineral wealth, combined with a relatively stable labour situation where strikes are rare and unemployment minimal, paves the way for even greater development at an ever-increasing pace. Indeed, some economists have predicted that South Africa may well become a major international power.

South Africa's achievement in engineering, technology, science, mining and agriculture is fast becoming recognised in the Western world. Dramatic breakthroughs in medicine have made her a world leader in this field. Perhaps symbolic of the Republic's rapid development is Johannesburg. This city, non-existent a mere 90 years ago, today resembles a mini-New York – vibrant, booming and very much part of the 20th century.

Over 600 000 industrialists, tourists and settlers entered South Africa in 1973. As the opportunities and the attractions of this unusually beautiful, exciting and interesting country become better known worldwide, these numbers are bound to increase manifold. Also, although part of Africa, and offering everything one expects to find in Africa, South Africa boasts many magnificent hotels and every possible service and amenity one would expect to find in a Westernized country.

The outstanding photographs in this book give a foretaste of the magnificent countryside, the peoples, animals, birds, flowers, precious stones – of nature's bounties to one of the most blessed countries on earth. Clearly set out, titled and concisely written will be found short historical sketches, information on ethnic groups, systems of government, the process of law and political parties. Under appropriate headings are described climatic conditions, vegetation, mineral resources, trade and industry.

It is my hope that overseas readers will find this book interesting enough to motivate the unforgettable experience of a visit to South Africa. Likewise, that it will influence many South Africans to see and learn more about their own beautiful country.

South Africa offers the best of all worlds: the 20th century in throbbing and vital cities and industries; the tranquillity of rural living and traditional hospitality; nature unspoilt in well-conserved game parks. And, to add to all these attractions, the unique and happy adventure of meeting peoples, Black, Brown and White. Some stem from the West, some from the East, but millions, some urbanised and some still tribalised, are all true children of Mother Africa.

Arnold Helfet. May 1975

Map of Africa circa 1351.

South Africa: History

Discovery of Southern Africa

As recently as 500 years ago European cartographers had no knowledge of what existed in Africa south of the equator. Navigators venturing down uncharted seas along its west coast envisaged that the continent flattened out south of the Ivory Coast. In fact they anticipated being able to sail east from Guinea along this 'flat coast' and thus to discover the legendary Christian kingdom of Abyssinia. From there they dreamed of reaching 'India-in-Africa' by proceeding still further east.

The pious Infante Dom Henrique, 'Henry the Navigator' of Portugal (1394 – 1460), dedicated his life to the spread of Christianity to these unknown lands and peoples. He planned to trade in spices, silks, ivory and slaves in order to amass the great wealth he required for the fight against the enemies of Christianity. He equipped expeditionary fleets commanded by personally chosen men. It was these Portuguese adventurers who were the first Europeans to discover Southern Africa. And they left proof for posterity of their landings and their Christianity by erecting an inscribed padrao (granite cross) to commemorate each new discovery. Some of their names are still used, Saldanha Bay and Cape Agulhas for example.

The ultimate purpose of these voyages, however, was to find a sea route from Europe to India and the East. As part of the enterprise they established convenient resting, revictualing and hospitalization ports of call en route. Thus were the beginnings of

7

Prince Henry the Navigator.

Bartholomew Diaz.

Vasco da Gama.

The Cape of Good Hope and its inhabitants in 1626.

Francisco de Almeida and compatriots do battle with Hottentots.

Angola on the south-west and Mozambique on the south-east coasts of Africa. Portugal did not establish 'presences' on any of the coastal areas which are presently South West Africa and the Republic of South Africa.

Curiously, as far back as 1493, Pope Alexander VI issued his celebrated Bull dividing the world's unknown lands between Portugal and Spain. By this decree Africa south of the known and settled countries became Portugal's domain.

During that period Portugal had also discovered South America and established Brazil, today one of the largest and most prosperous countries in the world. In retrospect it was possibly but a quirk of history that motivated Portugal not to colonise South Africa as did the Dutch some decades later. On March 1, 1510 Francisco de Almeida, Viceroy of Portuguese India, was killed in Table Bay together with 57 compatriots. They had anchored for water and become involved in a quarrel with local Hottentots. This incident, plus the loss of valuable ships wrecked on these stormy southern coasts, possibly influenced Lisbon in deciding against costly colonisation plans. Had the reverse occurred and Holland been forestalled, the enormous and contiguous territories from Angola round South West and South Africa right up to Mozambique could well have become a rich and powerful African Brazil with Portuguese as its only language.

But from fantasy back to facts, and to the beginning. One hundred and sixty-seven years were to pass between the first landing in Southern Africa and the establishment of the first settlement at the Cape of Good Hope.

Unlike the histories of the old European and Eastern countries, the story of South Africa contains comparatively few dates, few dynasties with noble names and few wars to chronicle. In fact, in those first 167 years, only ten events actually made historical headlines.

In 1485 a Portuguese nobleman of humble birth, Diego Cao, landed at Cape Cross on the barren coast of the Namib Desert.

Portuguese explorers raising a padrão.

His countryman Bartholomew Diaz was next to step on shore, this time further south at Walvis Bay on December 8, 1487. Soon after, he visited Lüderitz. Nine months later, in 1488, Diaz made his historic voyage round the Cape, but the only part of the peninsula he actually sighted was Cape Point.

King Manuel I, who ruled Portugal till 1521 and whose reign saw a vast growth of his trading empire, extending from Brazil to the Malayan Archipelago, elected Vasco da Gama to command the ships that were finally to reach India via the Cape. Meanwhile da Gama landed at St Helena Bay on November 7, 1497. In this first encounter between Europeans and Hottentots, the indigenous Brown people, he and three of his men were wounded. Nineteen days later his ships anchored at Mossel Bay, and on Christmas Day 1497 Vasco da Gama discovered Natal – hence its name.

Another 'first' occurred on that voyage. When da Gama's expedition landed at the mouth of the Limpopo River on January 6, 1498 they were to see southern Black people for the first time, probably a Tsonga tribe.

In 1503 Antonio de Saldanha, commander of a squadron en route to the East, sailed, through a navigational error, into what is now Table Bay. He climbed Table Mountain to become the first White man to see both the Indian and Atlantic oceans from this famous vantage point.

During this period Dutch and British ships used these southern harbours, but the future control of the Cape was to be determined as a result of the foundation in 1602 of the Dutch East India Company in the Netherlands. Originally this Company had no intention of establishing a settlement, as was happening at that time with the North American English colonies. But, in fact, its formation did lead within five decades to the birth of a new nation and the development of a country with vast natural and human resources, situated in one of the most strategic areas of the globe.

The first Dutch settlement

Jan van Riebeeck, a man of 32, sailed into Table Bay on April 6, 1652 to become the first Commander of the Cape. His mandate from the Dutch East India Company's powerful Council of Seventeen, Here XVII, was to tame the wild Table Valley, build a defensive fort, a hospital, and to provide fresh vegetables and meat for passing fleets. He was to keep peaceful relations with the primitive Hottentot cattle breeders and to barter with them for urgently needed meat.

Van Riebeeck was soon to discover, however, that the Hottentots were troublesome and unreliable trading partners. He thus found it expedient as early as 1657 to release from service some of his 90 'soldiers'. They were granted land for farming to supplement produce from the gardens he had established as an early priority. These 'freeburghers' thereby inaugurated the agricultural tradition, a tradition which was for centuries to be the backbone of this land of many farmers or *boers* – the Dutch appellation which is still proudly used and which has become synonymous with Afrikaner.

A year later a shipload of Black slaves from a captured Portuguese vessel brought a new dimension to the White and Brown inhabitants of the Cape. Thereafter the importation of slave labour from Madagascar, Mozambique and the East Indies continued until 1803, and slavery as such was formally abolished in 1834. All these infusions of foreign blood were to add an important element to the population and to the social relationships between servants and their employers in the years to come. In fact, from the seed of White, Brown and Black were to stem the original ancestors of the large, talented and Westernized population groups which, together with the Malay immigrants, are now known collectively as the Coloureds.

During its early years the small settlement wrestled with many problems, not made easier by the prevailing and violent south-east winds which devastated the farmlands. Poor crops

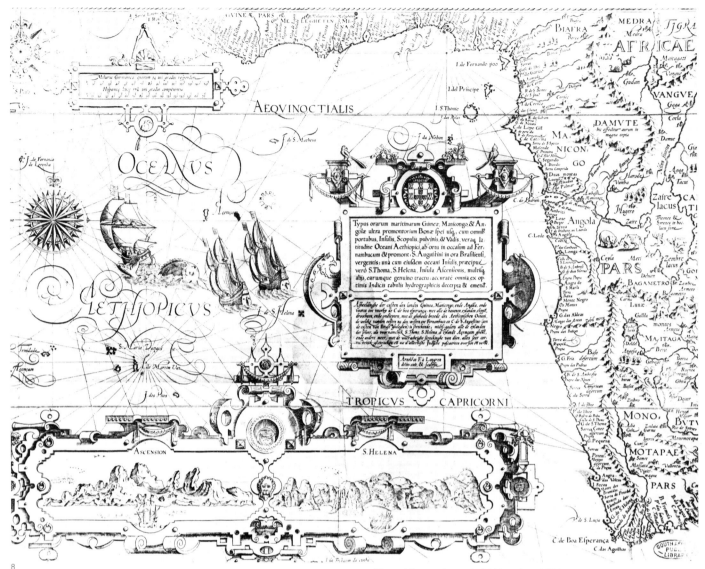

Map of the west coast of Africa circa 1600.

Jan van Riebeeck.

and frustration led inevitably to searches for more sheltered and better conditions. Thus, by 1700, a process of expansion into the immediate interior was in full swing. This movement or *trek* to larger and more suitable land continued until far into the 19th century by which time the borders of the present Republic had been reached and established.

During 1679 to 1707 two enterprising Governors, Simon van der Stel (Stellenbosch was named after him) and his son, Wilhem Adriaen, were to transpose the Colony from a state of chronic under-production to one of massive over-production, particularly of wheat and wine. In fact for the whole of the 18th century, surpluses to market absorption were to plague the pioneers who had so successfully established a viable agricultural economy.

Among the immigrants Simon van der Stel introduced to augment the freeburghers was a group of about 150 French Huguenot refugees who arrived around 1688. Although so small

Van Riebeeck's 'Fort de Goede Hoop'.

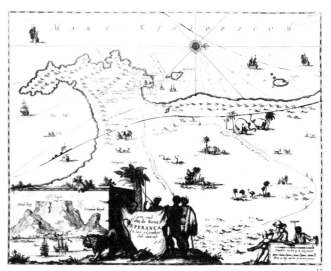

Map of the Western Cape circa 1665.

Hottentots at the Cape.

in number, they formed approximately 17% of the total White community. Religious Calvinists from a superior social background, they made a valuable and lasting contribution to the life and culture of the future Afrikaner people. Many of their descendants still proudly bear their family names – as also do those of German origin, who likewise settled at the Cape in the employ of the Dutch East India Company.

Simon van der Stel intended confining the Colony to the first surrounding mountain ranges and its activities to the soil. But the younger van der Stel encouraged cattle farming and spontaneous treks into the hinterland in search of water, good grazing and hunting grounds took place.

At this time the first real clash occurred between the Colonists and those in authority. In 1707 Governor Wilhem van der Stel was dismissed after a conflict with Stellenbosch farmers. They had bitterly opposed his high-handed policies and complained to Holland about his monopolistic control of the restricted market for farm produce in favour of his own interests and those of his friends.

The eventual price of this burgher victory was to prove very high and to have an historically adverse effect on the entire future of the new nation. Although more farmers were needed to satisfy the needs of the Company's ships, all sponsored immigration from Europe was stopped. Instead, additional slave labour was imported. These decisions largely account for the relatively small White population in South Africa to this day as compared, for example, with North America, where similar circumstances existed at the time.

Even though the number of Colonists doubled every 30 years, by the time the Company disappeared in 1795, 143 years after van Riebeeck's arrival, the White population totalled a meagre 15 000 souls who were thinly scattered over an area about one half that of the present Cape Province.

The last years of the Company

Eighteenth century Cape history, until about 1780 when the Afrikaner cattle farmers first encountered Black people in the area of the Fish River, was relatively uneventful. The sparse Hottentot population had shown comparatively little hostility towards the Colonists and, in fact, soon became a voluntary labour force. In contrast, the small groups of nomadic hit-and-run

Bushmen were troublesome, although they had not impeded the advance inland. These little yellow-skinned Stone Age people had always lived by hunting, and cattle-thieving from the White farmers proved even easier and more profitable. They used their deadly poison arrows to kill for food and they retreated reluctantly before the advancing White civilization which they could not understand.

However, the Black peoples were to prove an entirely different proposition. They were large in number and their age-old cultures and moral codes differed vastly from those of the Whites and of the Brown Hottentots and Bushmen. But it was common interests which were to cause bloodshed and trouble between Black and White; both were cattle owners and both were ever in search of fresh grazing territories.

By 1769 the Afrikaners had very thinly populated some 170 000 km² stretching mainly eastwards from the Cape. When

An early view of Stellenbosch.

they discovered the fertile Fish River Valley, the Black people they encountered there were the vanguard of tribes who for centuries had been gradually migrating southwards from central Africa. They were Xhosa, spearhead of other tribes of the Nguni group, who were later to father the Zulu and Swazi nations of today.

The first clash between these Whites and Blacks in 1780 led to nine wars during the following century. These confrontations effectively checked the hitherto peaceful eastward occupation of the large farms 'leased' from the Company.

Back in the Dutch Company-governed older established districts of the Cape and Stellenbosch all had remained tranquil until, during the troubled years of the American Revolution, England and the Netherlands were at war for the first time in a century. During this war French soldiers, allies of the American colonies, were to be garrisoned in peaceful Cape Town for some years. Also the ferments which led to the French Revolution and a patriotic movement in Holland wafted to the Cape. 'Patriots' in and around Cape Town were unsuccessful in their attempts to obtain improved civil rights, but two inland districts, Graaff-Reinet and Swellendam, successfully staged bloodless revolts in 1795 against the bureaucratic inefficiency of the ailing Company.

Although these were short-lived republics, they were the seeds from which grew the spirit of independence which has pervaded the history of the Afrikaners since the 19th century and which triumphed and culminated in the declaration of the Republic of South Africa on May 31, 1961.

The Cape becomes British

In September 1795 the Cape of Good Hope surrendered to a British expeditionary force. The Colonists had acted on the instructions of the Prince of Orange, who had chosen exile in England when his country became the Batavian Republic under revolutionary France.

This first British occupation lasted eight uneventful years and in 1803 the Treaty of Amiens returned the Cape to the Dutch.

However, when the war against Napoleon was resumed, the British re-occupied the Cape temporarily in January 1806. And finally, at the peace settlement of 1814, it was formally ceded to Great Britain, and not sold, as has periodically been stated.

The British wrought changes in the hitherto lackadaisical system of rule used by the Dutch East India Company. The Cape became a Crown Colony governed by senior officials. As the population was almost entirely non-British until 1820, an unpopular policy of Anglicisation was applied in order to overcome the problems of communication between officials and burghers. It aimed at substituting English for Dutch in Government service and the law courts and reducing the use of Dutch in schools and churches.

The Afrikaners, other than in their religious services, accepted these measures as they had also accepted the dictates of the Dutch period. It was to be left to the more politically conscious English, who started arriving in 1820, to clamour not many years later for the constitutional reforms that were to follow.

In 1820 some 5 000 British immigrants arrived from post-Waterloo Britain to settle on the eastern frontier of the Colony. Their arrival influenced the future of South Africa in many ways. As they were to serve as a buffer in the dangerous Black confrontation zone, they were soon involved in the horrors of war side by side with their Afrikaner neighbours. It did not take many years before they were to condemn the bureaucracy of the officials in charge of the Colony and to demand a representative form of government. Through their concerted efforts the Cape Colony received a partly nominated Legislative Council in 1834, an elected Parliament with an Executive of officials in 1854, and a fully responsible government in 1872.

The British settlers also changed the former unilingual situation in the community by infusing spoken English as against the hitherto only 'official' English. Its usage spread as the English population grew in Cape Town, with the development of the new settler towns of Port Elizabeth and Grahamstown, by mid-century immigration into Natal and, after 1870, by the arrival of more

Gerald Cubitt Arnold Helfet

South Africa

Publisher's Note

In a country as vast and diverse as South Africa
it would be a near impossible task for one
photographer to obtain a sufficiently representative
and consistently outstanding selection of
photographs as was required for this book. For this
reason we invited numerous other photographers
to submit material. For their co-operation
and enthusiasm we wish to thank them sincerely.
A list appears on page 208.

Map of the Western Cape circa 1710.

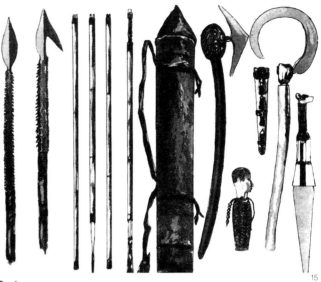

Bushman weapons.

immigrants who poured into the interior after the discovery of gold and diamonds. It was the English, too, who fought for and won the freedom of the press – a concept so cherished in their homeland.

The Great Trek

The instability of the Fish River frontier area and wars with Xhosa tribes thrusting south-westwards were the greatest problems faced by the British after they occupied the Cape. These events provided added reason for the dramatic northward migration to the interior by the Boers.

The Great Trek of 1835 – 37, which added the word *trek* to many foreign dictionaries, was a turning-point in South African history and one of the outstanding events of the 19th century. Boer frontier families totalling thousands of men, women and children, abandoned their farms and homes to brave the hardships of the unchartered interior, using sturdy, cumbersome ox-wagons. They had decided, despite great personal sacrifices and risk, to get as far away as possible from their British rulers under whom they saw no future for themselves or their children.

Some trekked round the southernmost Black tribes in the Eastern Cape and reached sub-tropical Natal where, in 1824, a small pioneer group of English traders had settled at the port now called Durban. Many moved north to cross the Orange River boundary of the Cape Colony and the highveld plateau south and north of the Vaal River. Others continued ever northwards to the Limpopo River, or westwards to the Kalahari semi-desert.

In the decades that followed, these intrepid trekkers were to establish the vast provinces of today's Orange Free State and Transvaal.

Traversing enormous distances over inhospitable country, these hardy pioneers had to combat many natural hazards; heat and droughts, colds and floods, deadly diseases and wild animals. They also had to fight for their lives and their livestock against two Black despots who, before the trekkers' advent, had decimated the other Black peoples in their paths. The first was Mzilikazi, a refugee Zulu general who, with his Matabele tribe,

dominated the high plateau. The second, Dingane, King of the Zulu, ruled Natal north of the Tugela River with strict discipline.

By 1839 the Voortrekkers had subdued both and were able to establish the Boer states of the Orange Free State and Natal.

Brit and Boer – Colonies and Republics

The first Boer Republic of Natal on the Indian Ocean coast was shortlived. Founded in 1839, it was annexed four years later by the British authorities who had continued to regard the trekkers as British subjects.

Similarly in 1846 the British established a resident official in Bloemfontein to 'govern' the emigrants between the Orange and Modder Rivers and to 'control' the wily Moshoeshoe, Chief of mountainous Basutoland.

However, it took but a few years before the British reversed the burdensome policy of responsibility for these far-flung areas and divergent peoples. By 1852 the Boers in the Transvaal were given their independence and, by a convention ratified at Bloemfontein in February 1854, independence was given also to the land between the Orange and Vaal Rivers. The latter became the Boer Republic of the Orange Free State, which remained independent until conquered by Britain 50 years later.

In 1854, too, the Cape Colony obtained its historic first elected Parliament. Responsible government followed in 1872, the first Cape Cabinet being elected from its members. This body, modelled on British parliamentary forms, was to be the forerunner of democratic rule in a united South Africa.

Thus the events triggered by the Great Trek led in less than 20 years to the division of South Africa into the two Boer Republics and the two British Colonies of the Cape and Natal. After 1850 Natal was to become predominantly English-speaking as a result of immigration from Britain, but its White numbers remained meagre compared with the very large Black population.

A new element was introduced into the already heterogeneous South African population when, in 1860, Natal introduced indentured Indian labourers for its sugar plantations. These

A fortified farm near the frontier.

Asians were not repatriated to their home country and, by 1900, their numbers had greatly increased, some settling also in the Cape and Transvaal. Their offspring today comprise a large and industrious group of citizens.

Numerous Black tribes had settled in and around the Republics and Colonies. Large numbers of Xhosa and other Nguni peoples lived in the eastern Cape and southern Natal; the Zulu were in the north of Natal; and a great arc of tribal settlements partially encircled the Boer Republics. The Bechuanaland or Kalahari side was scattered with Tswana tribes; in the north were the North Sotho and Venda; and to the east, near Portuguese Mozambique, were the Tsonga and the Swazi, who were neighbours of the militant Zulu. Inside the arc were pockets of South Sotho and the mountain fortress where the great Moshoeshoe had established the Basotho nation. This area, Basutoland, became a British colony, then a dependency of the Cape, again a British colony and, in 1966, the present independent state of Lesotho.

Diamonds and gold discovered

During most of the 19th century the small White populations in the Colonies and the Republics subsisted on an agricultural economy. Among their many problems were the maintenance of their European civilization and peaceful relations with the Black people, who lived by the age-old codes of primeval Africa. As a result, even in those early times, the respective White rulers were searching for some common approach to what, subsequently, became known as 'Bantu Policies'. This search still continues – for policies that will ensure the peaceful and prosperous coexistence of all South African ethnic groups.

While the Republics were making abortive attempts towards federation, either individually or including the Colonies, world-shattering events occurred which were to change South Africa from a pastoral country to an industrial giant. Between 1867 and 1871 spectacular discoveries of diamonds in the arid areas of Griqualand West drastically altered the economic and political scenes – as did similar discoveries in semi-desert northern Namaqualand in the late 1920s and early 1930s – bringing timely relief to South Africa in those depression and drought-haunted years.

Alluvial diggings along the Vaal River and fabulous volcanic pipes of 'blue ground' rich in diamonds at the new town of Kimberley were magnets that drew thousands of fortune hunters from all over the world.

Unfortunately the euphoria created by these discoveries was marred by bitter strife between the Boer Republics and numerous Griqua and Tswana chiefs over the ownership of the diamond fields. These disputes were abruptly ended by British imperialism. The diamond areas were annexed and created into the Crown Colony of Griqualand West. Britain then made diplomatic overtures to the Boer Republics to federate with her Colonies. When these failed, more forceful steps were then taken resulting in the annexation of the Transvaal in 1877.

The Boers, including Cape Colony Afrikaners, were enraged at this callous imperialism and all prospects of peaceful federation disappeared. Instead, these actions led to the outbreak of the First Anglo-Boer War in 1880. And, after the British suffered a humiliating defeat at the Battle of Majuba Hill, the Transvaal regained her independence in 1881.

The Majuba *débâcle* led also to spectacular Afrikaner poli-

Above: An early view of Port Elizabeth.
Left: The formal British takeover of the Cape in 1814.
Bottom left: Indian labourers arriving in Durban.

tical activity in the Cape. Men who had until then been comparatively passive spectators commenced playing decisive roles in
politics and Parliament. Under Jan Hendrik Hofmeyer (1845 –
1909) the Afrikaner Bond firmly established a new awareness
and participation in national affairs. This Afrikaner leadership was
soon to overtake that of the English politicians and, under the
illustrious Boer Generals Botha, Smuts and Hertzog, the British-
founded parliamentary system continued to flourish in South
Africa.

Returning to the era of the Republics – the 'Model Republic',
the Orange Free State, developed very successfully and pros-
perously under three great leaders: Presidents Brand (1863 –
88), Reitz (1888 – 95) and Steyn (1895 – 1902). The South African Republic, today's Transvaal, likewise went from strength to
strength particularly from 1883 to 1902 while under the legendary
President Paul Kruger. Both Republics were to return to British
rule when the Peace of Vereeniging sealed the end of the Second
Anglo-Boer War in 1902.

During those years of European colonialism the Germans,
too, decided to take a slice of Southern Africa. In 1884 they
surprised the British and the Republics by annexing territory one
and a half times the size of Germany on the west coast north of
the Orange River. Thereby German South West Africa was established, and for 30 years the territory was ruled by German officials. After the outbreak of World War I in 1915 South African
forces under General Louis Botha conquered the territory which,
as a result of the Treaty of Versailles and the decision of the
Council of the League of Nations, was placed under South African mandatory rule. In recent years strong pressures have been
exerted by a majority of states in the United Nations for South

Right: Moshoeshoe.
Below: The first sale of sugar in Durban in 1856.
Bottom: Digging for diamonds.

Africa to relinquish control of this fast-developing and potentially wealthy country.

The discovery of the world's richest gold-bearing reef on the Witwatersrand in 1886 was another great history-making event in South Africa during the last two decades of the 19th century.

Rail links were built during the nineties to join coastal ports with Johannesburg and Pretoria and aliens, the so-called *Uitlanders* used these convenient trains in their stampede to the new El Dorado.

Cecil John Rhodes, diamond magnate of Kimberley, empire-builder and Prime Minister of the Cape Colony from 1890 to 1895, was bitterly opposed to Paul Kruger whose independent Transvaal he saw as the only obstacle in his plan to unite the whole of Southern Africa under British rule.

He used some of the British treasure-seekers on the Reef in the notorious and unsuccessful Jameson Raid of 1895 – 96 into the Transvaal in an attempt to overthrow the Kruger Government.

The operation failed, Jameson and his backers were discredited, but its aftermath of tension and bitterness inevitably led to war a few years later.

Anglo-Boer War II

Rhodes' hopes to create a British federation from the Cape to the Zambezi were shattered by the collapse of the Jameson Raid. The further execution of Tory policy towards South Africa thus reverted to Colonial Secretary, Joseph Chamberlain, and High Commissioner, Sir Alfred Milner. Tensions between Brit and Boer continued to mount despite concessions offered by the Transvaal's President Kruger, the Orange Free State's President Steyn and British officials, in earnest efforts to prevent the tragedy of armed conflict. But all these negotiations failed and the Second Anglo-Boer War broke out on October 11, 1899.

It was a strange and sad war between completely disparate antagonists. The British soldiers commanded by professional officers were more accustomed to conventional battle formations and operations. They wore uniforms distinguishable from afar and unsuited to the open South African veld and fluctuating climatic conditions.

The Boers were familiar with the terrain of their country and were excellent horsemen and marksmen. These factors proved of utmost importance in a war in which machine-guns were to play a minor role and static trench-warfare was as yet unknown. Even the fact that the Boer farmer-soldiers had hardly any real uniforms was to prove a very useful camouflage.

For 32 long, bitter and bloody months the might of the British Empire was, astonishingly, held at bay by the relatively small number (52 000 boys and men from 18 to 60 years of age) of ill-armed Boers. They had operated as commandos – a word adopted ever since in the war terminology of many languages – under guerilla tacticians whose names were to become legend. Leaders among them were Christiaan de Wet, Koos de la Rey, Louis Botha, Christiaan Beyers and Jan Smuts. Smuts was years later again to cover himself in glory, this time as an ally to former enemy, Britain, during World Wars I and II.

With the assistance of Afrikaner rebels in the Cape Colony and Natal, Boer commandos harassed the British from the Atlantic to the Indian seaboards. But overwhelming numbers, superior arms and transport facilities plus grievous losses finally ended

President Paul Kruger.

British forces retreat from Majuba Hill.

the unequal struggle. The Boer Generals laid down their arms and reluctantly signed the Treaty of Vereeniging on May 31, 1902. This concluded an epic conflict which had evoked worldwide sympathy for the Boers.

The war had left farms and villages in the Republics in ruins, their livestock decimated and their populations devastatingly reduced – approximately 26 000 civilians lost their lives, mainly from illness in concentration camps, plus 5 000 in battle. Britain, too, from about half a million men suffered 98 000 casualties – 7 000 dead – and her treasury was stripped by £191 000 000 sterling.

However, like the Great Trek, the event was to reshape the history of South Africa and its peoples. All the land between German South West in the west and Portuguese Mozambique in the north-east henceforth became British South Africa. The disappearance of the independent Republics paved the way for a closer political union, a union that had been attempted unsuccessfully so often before.

Another side result of the war was the stimulus it gave to Afrikaner nationalism and the entry of republican-minded Afrikaners into wider South African politics. Likewise, it also gave a great fillip to the firm establishment of the young Afrikaans language, which soon thereafter gained equal status with English to make the country officially bilingual in 1925.

The Union of South Africa

The eight years between 1902 and 1910 saw widespread reconstruction and reconciliation between Boer and Brit. The gold-mining industry was revived, problems of the railways and customs tariffs between the four colonies resolved and the war-impoverished farmers rehabilitated. During 1906 and 1907 the British Liberal Government granted responsible government to the two former Republics. And thus colonial Parliaments under Boer leadership came into being alongside the older Cape and Natal Parliaments.

In turn the bitter enemies of a few years earlier sat together in 1908 – 9 to draft a Bill which was passed by the British Parliament as *The South Africa Act.* This defined the constitution of the Union of South Africa and took effect from May 31, 1910. Thus was born, exactly eight years after the war, a new self-governing Dominion, which took its place alongside the older Dominions of Canada, New Zealand and Australia.

The 1910 Constitution and form of government, with the exception of some minor amendments, remained virtually unchanged until the birth of the Republic of South Africa on May 31, 1961, exactly 51 years later, and the main features of this constitution exist to this day.

Excluded from the Union of South Africa were the three High Commission Territories of Basutoland (now Lesotho), Bechuanaland (now Botswana) and Swaziland. Rhodesia was also excluded. Today all these territories are independent and self-governing.

The Age of the Generals begins

General Louis Botha (1862 – 1919) was the first and very popular and successful Prime Minister of the Union of South Africa. In his Cabinet were two other Boer Generals who were to succeed him as Prime Ministers: Jan Christiaan Smuts (1870 – 1950), brilliant,

Cecil John Rhodes.   25

General Joubert : Commandant-   26
General of the Boer forces.

intellectual and a Cambridge law graduate; and James Barry Munnik Hertzog (1866 – 1942), Doctor of Laws and former Orange Free State Judge.

In the newly-united South Africa, diamonds and gold still dominated an economy formerly based on agriculture. This also brought about a population shift as many rural Afrikaners drifted from the *platteland* (rural areas) to the towns. In fact between 1911 and 1936 the percentage of Whites living in the cities rose from 31% to 48% of the total White population of the country. This influx, which accelerated even more after World War II, unsettled the social and economic situation generally. It was to create a 'poor White' problem which was only resolved eventually by rapid and countrywide industrialisation following the two World Wars.

Despite excellent legislative achievements by the Botha Cabinet, there were early signs of dissension from two quarters in the new government: General Hertzog, fighting for the preservation and development of Afrikaner culture and identity, feared the Botha-Smuts policy of conciliation with the English elements. And, outside of parliamentary politics, White labour had been organised by the eloquent leader of the Labour Party, Colonel Creswell, who was dissatisfied with the existing working conditions.

As a result, early in 1913–14, Hertzog formed the National Party and went into the political wilderness in opposition to Botha. Also in 1914 White mineworkers on the Rand, railwaymen and coal miners, were involved in a general strike. Smuts, as Minister of Defence, subdued their leaders by force and deportation and consequently, outraged Labour became a political force for the first time.

World War I broke out in August 1914 and the conflagration in Europe had a profound effect on and in South Africa. Britain was at war with Germany and South Africa was part of her Empire. At Britain's request the Botha Government launched an attack on German South West and with hardly any losses occupied Windhoek, the capital, during May 1915. The whole territory of 825 000 km² fell under South African military control. After the war it became a mandated territory to be administered by the Union of South Africa.

In 1916 General Smuts led a campaign against the Germans in Tanganyika (Tanzania). He conquered it on Britain's behalf and then remained in Britain until 1919 as counsellor to Lloyd George's Government.

At home anti-British elements among the Afrikaner population, led by General Hertzog, became more and more estranged from Generals Botha and Smuts. Smuts in particular had personally contributed during the war years to the formulation of the British Commonwealth and to South Africa's enhanced status as an equal and autonomous Dominion in the new grouping of 'British' nations. This, too, while making him a popular statesman in Britain, added the more to his unpopularity among his nationalism-minded fellow Afrikaners.

Smuts becomes Prime Minister

General Botha died in 1919 and Smuts automatically succeeded him as Prime Minister. Despite a period of apparent prosperity from 1915 to 1920, his Government ran into many difficulties due partly to post-war inflation. Thus, in the March 1920 general election, Smuts' South African Party (SAP) won four fewer seats than the Nationalists and had to depend on Sir Thomas Smartt's Unionists for an overall majority over the Nationalists and the 21 Labour members. This unsatisfactory situation resulted in the calling of another election in February 1921 when Smuts emerged with a strong working majority.

However, even his new Government was soon beset with many serious difficulties. Prices had collapsed worldwide, South Africa abandoned the gold standard, low-grade mines were closed, agriculture faced ruin and unemployment became a major problem.

In 1922 Smuts proclaimed martial law to curb vandalism. White mine-workers went on strike due to ill-feeling regarding Bantu labour and bloodshed was rife. He also suffered biting criticism over the tough methods he had used to quell these upheavals and the rebellion of the Bondelswarts Hottentot tribe in South West Africa. Partly to counteract the growing opposition to his Government, Smuts urgently attempted to persuade Southern Rhodesia to join the Union. Nevertheless, in a referendum in October 1922, Rhodesia elected to go its own way as a self-governing colony – as she did again in her UDI declaration of 1965, but then not as a colony.

Hertzog heads Pact Government

By June 1924 the sands had run out for the SAP Government. Smuts had called another election after losing an important by-election at Wakkerstroom, and a new Government, comprising a Nationalist and Labour 'pact', ousted Smuts with a combined 80 seats against his 54.

Hertzog became Prime Minister, the third of the Boer Generals to lead a Union Government. His Cabinet of ten included three Labourites and for the next five years the economy of the country prospered under Finance Minister N. C. Havenga. Havenga had

General Louis Botha and his family.

returned South Africa to the gold standard and produced surplus budgets; the production of diamonds soared as a result of new discoveries in the Western Transvaal and fabulous and spectacular finds in the sandy Namaqualand coastal strip south of the Orange River mouth.

Industrial development in this period was given an enormous fillip when, in March 1928, the State-controlled South African Iron and Steel Industrial Corporation (ISCOR) was established in Pretoria. This giant undertaking, one of the largest of its kind in the world today, went into production in 1934. It has ever since exploited the country's vast resources of coal and iron ore and made South Africa largely self-sufficient in the production of steel.

The Hertzog era was noted for many bitter parliamentary struggles involving his four Bills on legislation for what he called 'segregation' for Bantu, Indian and Coloured citizens. The strong SAP opposition, which still held a Senate majority, defeated these measures, which were to be reintroduced some years later.

Two issues, however, were settled: the first, amicably, was the acceptance of Afrikaans as an official language; the second, after acrimonious and dour debate, the final compromise design of a new flag. This colourful but controversial design remains the national flag, but there is resistance to the inclusion of the Union Jack and some still hope and plan to replace it with a 'truly South African' flag in the future.

Depression and Coalition

At the end of five years of 'Pact' Government the National Party won the 1929 general election with an overall majority of seven. Hertzog retained the Labour partnership, however, although Creswell had won only eight seats.

Also in 1929 the disastrous Wall Street collapse in the USA plunged the world into economic chaos and depression, seriously crippling South Africa as well. Finance Minister N. C. Havenga further aggravated the position by stubbornly refusing to follow Britain in abandoning the gold standard. This led to continued pressure from the mining houses and the Smuts Opposition, ever falling prices of agricultural products and, finally, a wild flight of capital in anticipation of the eventual and inevitable dropping of the gold standard.

The dilemma created for Hertzog and Havenga by these desperate crises reached a climax when their former Cabinet Minister colleague, Judge Tielman Roos, dramatically re-entered politics in December 1932. Roos urged the end of the gold standard and advocated the formation of an all-party national government in order to save the country from ruin. His advent had the dramatic impact anticipated, but not his planned re-entry results. Smuts offered the hand of friendship to his political enemy, Hertzog, and before the end of 1932 the gold standard was abandoned. Hertzog and Smuts agreed on a coalition programme and a strangely amicable general election took place in May 1933 with old foes assisting each other.

The election result found Hertzog as Prime Minister, Smuts his Deputy, and their following in the House a massive 138 members with only 6 in opposition. In December 1934 the United South African National Party was formed (today's United Party) and the South African Party ceased to exist. Dr D. F. Malan, not satisfied that coalition was in the interest of the Afrikaner cause, went into opposition and kept the National Party alive, although with only 19 seats. Fourteen years and a war later, he was to become Prime Minister and his party the Government.

The coalition years of 1934 to 1939 brought South Africa great prosperity, progress, racial harmony, economic growth and political peace.

The hoisting of the Union Jack at Windhoek.

28

But clouds had started gathering, when, in 1938, the prospects of war in Europe crystallised conflicting political views in South Africa. Hertzog insisted that South Africa remain neutral; Smuts maintained that the Union, as a British ally, should join in any conflict with Hitler's Germany. War was declared on September 3, 1939. The next day in a dramatic debate Hertzog, with support from Malan, lost the vote on neutrality by 67 to 80. South Africa was at war and Smuts, in his 70th year, became Prime Minister once more.

Smuts and World War II

The South African Army with 20 000 Whites in uniform in 1939, saw the end of the War in 1944 with armed forces totalling 350 000 – including 123 000 Coloureds and Africans in auxiliary services. South Africans served with distinction in four theatres: Ethiopia, North Africa, Italy and Madagascar. Three thousand lost their lives.

General Smuts, who was made a British Field-Marshal, became Churchill's valued counsellor, as he had been to Lloyd George during World War I. His international reputation as a soldier, tactician and statesman of world calibre, in 1945 earned him a prominent role in drafting the preamble to the Charter of the United Nations and in the foundation of the new world body.

However, at home Smuts, like Churchill in Britain, was losing support. Returned ex-servicemen had many grievances arising from post-war adjustments. Smuts' brilliant Deputy, Jan H. Hof-

General J. B. M. Hertzog.

29

General Jan Christiaan Smuts.

30

Police disperse strikers in Johannesburg.

meyer, ahead of his time in the South African context, was losing support by his forceful advocacy of a better deal for the non-Whites. And, in contrast, Dr Malan with the sympathy of Hertzog had formulated a policy of 'separateness' or *apartheid* for the White, Coloured, Indian and Black population groups which won him support from many White voters – Afrikaners in particular.

On May 26, 1948 Smuts' Government was defeated unexpectedly and sensationally: Malan won 70 seats, Havenga added his nine, and together they outnumbered Smuts by a scant majority of five. Thus departed the last of the Boer General Prime Ministers. He died, disappointed and disillusioned, in September 1950 shortly after his 80th birthday.

Malan entrenches Nationalism

After this narrow victory in 1948 the National Party and its Afrikaner Government went from strength to strength. In 1949 their hotly disputed measure to admit six members from South West Africa to the Union House of Assembly was adopted by Parliament. All six voted with the Government, which is still the situation today.

The National Party has remained in power ever since, increasing its parliamentary strength in successive elections in 1953, 1958, 1961 and 1966, losing a few seats in 1970, and gaining a few in 1974. Dr Malan was succeeded as Prime Minister by Adv. J. G. Strydom in 1954 and by Dr H. F. Verwoerd in 1958. Under Verwoerd the Union became a Republic on May 31, 1961 after a narrow 52% to 48% referendum majority. This followed on South Africa's withdrawal from membership of the British Commonwealth only a few months earlier and proved to be the victorious culmination of an historical process and Afrikaner dream which had dated back to the early Dutch rule.

On September 6, 1966 Dr Verwoerd was assassinated in Parliament by a temporary messenger who was subsequently committed to a mental institution. He was succeeded as Prime Minister by B. J. Vorster, the Minister of Justice in his Cabinet.

SOUTH AFRICA TODAY
Parliament in 1974

During the spectacular rise of the National Party between 1948 and 1974 the official Opposition, other than making a few gains in 1970, lost ground in every election. After Smuts' death in 1950, Adv. J. G. N. Strauss became leader and he was succeeded in 1956 by Sir De Villiers Graaff, son of a member of the first Union Cabinet.

Twelve prominent members of the UP resigned from the Party in 1959 as a result of irreconcilable disagreement over its race policies. They established the more liberally orientated Progressive Party under leadership of Dr Jan Steytler MP. Two years later, in the 1961 election, only one of the 12 retained a parliamentary seat for the new party. She was Helen Suzman, MP for Houghton, who alone carried the Progressive Party flag

Dr D. F. Malan. 32

Adv. J. G. Strydom. 33

Dr H. F. Verwoerd. 34

Prime Minister B. J. Vorster. 35

until the general election in 1974. Then, under the leadership of Colin Eglin, six more seats were won by the Progressives, all at the expense of the United Party. Since the 1974 elections four United Party MPs, under the leadership of Harry Schwarz, broke away from the United Party and formed the Reform Party.

The new Parliament in 1974 thus comprised: National Party 123 seats, United Party 37 seats, Progressives 7 seats and Reform Party 4 seats.

The Present and the Future

Since World War II many global changes have occurred, but nowhere have these been more dramatic than in Africa. As the European colonial powers hastily withdrew from the African Continent and granted independence to country after country, so the more and more did Southern Africa come under world scrutiny and pressure for change. And when in 1974 Portugal, too, decided to give her African territories their independence by 1975, only Rhodesia, South West Africa and South Africa remained under White rule.

The Republic of South Africa is of course neither a colony nor attached to any colonial power. She is a rich, powerful, industrialised, and Western-orientated country. Her official currency, the Rand, is one of the most stable in the world and she has trading partners in most corners of the globe.

Nevertheless South Africa has for many years been Africa's odd-man-out. She has few friends in the United Nations and is excluded from participation in the Olympic Games and from international sporting activities in many spheres. This unpopularity springs mainly from the fact that, unlike in other African countries, South Africa's White minority of 3 800 000 rules over a total population of 21 500 000 (1970 Census) Black, Brown and White citizens. Her Separate Development *(apartheid)* and separate Black Homelands policies are either criticised or condemned. However, she is admired, albeit secretly, for having maintained a largely peaceful existence and stable growth, while just the opposite has occurred in so many of the countries that are her most vociferous critics.

Since 1974, soft voices have been heard and moves have been initiated for détente and peace between Southern Africa and its northern neighbours. If these winds of change blow friendship and co-operation, the Republic of South Africa has much to offer in expertise, assistance, food and trade to the underdeveloped countries that so desperately need to improve the lot of their own peoples.

The history of South Africa contains many stories. Some are grim and ugly, many are beautiful and exciting, all are fascinating.

THE PEOPLES OF THE REPUBLIC OF SOUTH AFRICA

A kaleidoscope of the colourful and diverse peoples that compose the population of the Republic of South Africa can be studied by spending but a few hours on Cape Town's Grand Parade – the most interesting times being Wednesday and Saturday mornings, when the 'flea market' operates.

This large square was levelled as a parade-ground in 1697 and has been used ever since for military occasions, historic events, as a market-place and as a favourite tourist attraction. Exotic fruits, vegetables, masses of beautiful wild and cut flowers and herbs from nearby mountain slopes are offered for sale by Asian and Coloured men and women, among whom are many characters who 'entertain' with inimitable *Kaapse* (Cape) mannerisms and patois. Trestle-tabled displays of bric-a-brac occupy a large area of the square. Motley crowds mill around and barter with the traders, and among them all are to be found a variety of the peoples who are South Africans. Whites, Nordic-pale or suntanned brown; Coloureds, some light complexioned others dark; Blacks of many features and from many tribes; Asians and Cape Malays: they all belong to this vast country, lapped by the Atlantic and Indian oceans which meet near this 'Tavern of the Seas'.

According to 1970 census figures the Republic, including the areas designated as Black Homelands, then had a population of 21 402 470. Of these, 15 036 360 were Blacks, 3 726 540 Whites, 2 021 430 Coloureds and 618 140 Asians.

The Black People

South of an imaginary line drawn across the waist of Africa from the west coast south of Nigeria to approximately the mouth of the Tana River on the East coast, the population of the sub-continent, with the exception of minority groups such as Khoisans (Brown peoples), Whites, Coloureds and Asiatics, consists almost entirely of dark people collectively referred to as *Bantu.*

During many centuries, but from the 16th to the 19th in particular, while the 'Old World' was discovering and colonising the Americas and Southern Africa. numerous Black tribes in central Africa were likewise searching for pastures anew far from their traditional homes.

Originally settled in the region of the Great Lakes of Central East Africa, they moved southwards in successive waves as climatic conditions and tribal conflicts made their own territories untenable. These migrations were to be dramatised in history only when Black and White met for the first time in Southern Africa. On January 6, 1498 Vasco da Gama landed at the mouth of the Limpopo River and saw a tribe of Black people – the first recorded Black and White meeting south of the Equator. However, the first actual confrontation took place when the paths of Black and White crossed and clashed at the Fish River Valley in the Eastern Cape in 1780.

These dark peoples are primarily of mixed Hamitic and Negroid descent. Although referred to as Bantu, this term is a linguistic rather than a racial concept. Many now prefer to be called Africans or simply Blacks. The belief, widely held in the West, that all Blacks belong to a single homogeneous people or ethnic entity, is completely erroneous. In customs, traditions and language the Zulus, for example, differ as much from the Tswanas as the French differ from the Italians.

The migrations of the Black peoples, whose descendants live in Southern Africa today, were massive both in numbers and distances and were canalised into five main streams. Over the centuries these were further fragmented by bloody intertribal conflicts under despotic warlords and by the absorption of weaker tribes by stronger. They have crystallised into seven distinct Black groups speaking ten different interrelated languages. In 1970 their numbers were:

Zulu	4 026 082
Xhosa	3 929 922
Tswana	1 718 508
Pedi (North Sotho)	1 603 530
Southern Sotho	1 453 354
Shangaan-Tsonga	736 978
Swazi	498 704
Venda	357 875
South Ndebele	232 922
North Ndebele	181 719

These Blacks form but part of about 70 million people who live in the southern half of Africa and speak roughly 200 related Bantu languages or dialects.

About half of South Africa's Blacks live and work outside the Homelands – in cities, towns, villages and farms throughout all four Provinces. And it is estimated that roughly 1 million of these 7½ million are resident in one Black township, Soweto, near Johannesburg. In comparison, the Whites in Greater Johannesburg number roughly half a million.

The other half of the 15 000 000 Blacks live in the areas

Sir De Villiers Graaff. 36   Colin Eglin. 37

designated by Bantu Acts as their 'traditional Homelands'. These Homelands have been the subject of White political controversy and Black-White confrontation and disagreement since Union. Under the *Bantu Land Act of 1913* 9,2 million hectares of land were reserved for exclusive Bantu occupation. A subsequent Act in 1936 earmarked another 6,2 million hectares for this purpose. The 15,4 million hectares involved now form a motley pattern of over 20 areas, in all four Provinces, which it is intended will become consolidated into eight independent, self-governing states.

No Homeland has yet reached full independence, but the Transkei became self-governing in 1970 and expects to be the first to receive sovereign independence.

During 1972 seven others had achieved legislative status. They are (spoken languages given in brackets): the Ciskei (Xhosa), KwaZulu (Zulu), Lebowa (North Sotho), Venda (Chivenda), Gazankulu (Tsonga), Bophuthatswana (Tswana) and Basotho-Qwaqwa (South Sotho).

The rapid emergence of millions of these Black citizens from tribal life to Westernized urban and agricultural societies is a phenomenon which is possibly demonstrated more spectacularly in South Africa than anywhere else in the world. This is illustrated the more in that, by his labour and skills, the Black man has become an integral part of this highly industrialised country and has immeasurably contributed to its present development and prosperity.

The Whites

Most of the 3¾ million Whites are descendants of Dutch, French, British and German settlers – with smaller admixtures of other European peoples, mainly Portuguese, Greek and Italian. South Africa has two official languages and statistics reveal that over 60% of Whites are Afrikaners. Of these, approximately 50% use Afrikaans as their home language, 30% English and the remainder both Afrikaans and English. Most White South Africans are, however, bilingual.

Of this population group 93,8% claim membership of Christian churches. The largest following, 1 487 080, belongs to the Nederduitse Gereformeerde Kerk (Dutch Reformed Church)

Dr N. Diederichs,
South Africa's third State President.

Bantu Homelands.

while the three biggest other Christian denominations comprise Anglican Church 399 950, Methodist 357 410 and Roman Catholic 304 840. Many other Christian denominations are well represented. In addition, 118 000 belong to the Jewish faith.

The Afrikaners: Historically and culturally the Afrikaners are undoubtedly the most entrenched indigenous White community in Africa. Politically they are the most influential people in the southern subcontinent and theirs is the newest language in the world.

The Afrikaner stems from rural stock and was mainly responsible for the creation of the agricultural economy of this country. Today, however, more than 70% are urbanised and, whereas they had tended in the past to lag behind their English-speaking compatriots economically, educationally, in industry, commerce and mining, the margin of difference has shrunken rapidly.

Afrikaner participation in politics, the armed forces, police and in the civil service is numerically far greater than that of the English-speaking community. Afrikaans literature and theatre have taken enormous strides during this century and have added significant dimensions to the South African scene, as have the galaxy of artists whose works adorn galleries and homes both here and abroad.

The English-speaking: Ethnically not as homogeneous and demographically not as indigenous as the Afrikaners, the English-speaking population, numbering roughly 1,4 million, is mainly of British descent. Their greatest impact has been in the economic sphere, particularly in the industrial, commercial and mining sectors. They brought with them not only capital, but also technical skills and business know-how so essential to the foundation and progress of a newly developing country.

Because of their urban-industrial background, the English have mainly settled in urban centres – hence the pronounced English character of most South African cities. Resultantly also, the advanced technical culture of industrialised Britain is reflected in their contributions in the fields of housing, social security, urban planning, mass communication media, public administration, education, science, transport (the establishment of railways in particular) and the various professions.

The English group has had significant influence on all forms of art expression and many South African writers such as Sarah Gertrude Millin, Alan Paton, Roy Campbell, Nadine Gordimer – to name but a few – are internationally renowned.

In sport, the English introduced tennis, rugby, cricket and golf, in all of which South Africans (Springboks) have competed with distinction against the world's greatest.

Other Whites: About 30 000 immigrants, mostly from Europe, settle here annually. Many of those from the Continent retain, at least for a while, their home languages which include Dutch, French, Italian, Portuguese, Greek and German.

The cultures, culinary arts, industrious habits and technical skills of these Europeans, almost all of whom live in the cities, have enriched the already Westernized way of life of their country of adoption. Numbers of them own restaurants which specialise in the dishes of their countries.

A very small number of Whites do not belong to one of the Christian religious denominations. Of these, some hundreds are Islamic or Hindus and 118 000 Jewish.

Despite their small numbers Jews have played a significant role in the development of South Africa. They stem from British, German and Eastern European immigrants who arrived here from the early 19th century onwards. Their numbers were added to by refugees from the Nazi holocaust who established new lives in South Africa. Jews have contributed appreciably in business, industry and the arts and they have participated with distinction in civic and political life.

Kaizer Matanzima,
Paramount Chief of the Transkei.

Gatsha Buthelezi,
Paramount Chief of KwaZulu.

The Coloureds

In addition to the Blacks and Whites the Republic of South Africa is also the home of two other distinct population groups: the Coloured and Asian communities.

The Coloured people are of mixed ethnic descent and as a result heterogeneous in physical appearance. Their origin dates back to the Dutch settlement at the Cape in 1652. Among their forebears were the nomadic Khoisan tribes (mainly Hottentots, but also Bushmen), Black slaves from West Africa and the East Indies, and Europeans. Later there was also an admixture of Bantu blood.

Of the roughly 2 million Coloureds in 1970, 86,8% lived in the Cape Province, mainly in the Cape Peninsula and neighbouring districts. They include two subcultural groups, the Cape Malays and the Griquas. The Griquas, settled in the north-western and north-eastern Cape Province, are mainly of Hottentot-European ancestry and are gradually being absorbed into the rest of the Coloured community.

The Cape Malays, descendants of the early Muslim people introduced to the Cape by the Dutch East India Company from their colonies in the East, number under 150 000. They live almost entirely in the Cape Peninsula, many in the historic Malay Quarter in Cape Town. They remain faithful to the Islamic religion and traditions. Many of their tasty curry and spiced dishes have become traditional Cape fare. Besides being a colourful and musical people, they have made a great contribution particularly to the garment and building industries.

Ninety percent of all Coloureds are members of some Christian church and about the same percentage are Afrikaans-speaking.

The Coloured people are a songful community. They have an inherent love for music and a natural feeling for rhythm. Their culture is Western, their homes, food, dress and ways of life are like those of their White fellow-citizens. Originally people of the

soil, they have easily adapted to the 'machine age'. The men are employed in the fishing industry, as artisans – many thousands in building – in factories and in commerce. The women, deft and nimble with their hands, have established an indispensable niche for themselves in the large Cape clothing industry. And, as they further their educational qualifications, so are the men and women filling more and more important professional, business, teaching, nursing and clerical positions.

After a long struggle for recognition as equal citizens, the Coloured people yearn for, and are beginning to see, better years ahead.

The Asians

Mainly of Indian origin – the only major non-Indian group being the 6 000 Chinese – the Asian population in 1970 totalled 620 422. This is the largest group of Indian origin outside India and Pakistan, and more than all the Indians in the rest of Africa. Nearly 515 000 live in Natal within a radius of 150 km of Durban, where the first Indian immigrants landed in 1860.

The Indian community, both Hindu and Muslim, has retained its cultural and religious identity and rarely marries into other faiths. They are an industrious and diligent people, 96% of their children attending schools. Over 2 300 students are enrolled at the Indian University of Durban–Westville and many more in other universities and colleges.

The Indian community has established its own niche in the economic, social, educational and cultural spheres. And the pace and scope of its activities are increasing rapidly within the bounds of existing Government policy.

The Bushmen

Any account of the peoples of South Africa would be incomplete without mention of the Bushmen. These little yellow Stone Age people have been found scattered over parts of Southern Africa from the Cape to the Equator. They have been there for at least 12 000 to 15 000 years and some anthropologists believe that they may be the oldest living group which has remained unchanged and genetically 'pure' since primeval times.

It is estimated that these primitive Nimrods today total about 55 000 in the whole of Southern Africa and they are virtually confined to South West Africa, the arid Kalahari regions of Botswana and the northern Cape.

The Bushmen will, hopefully, be preserved from extinction in the face of the inexorable spread of Western civilization. However, they have immortalised themselves in the primitive rock art they have left for posterity as visual records of their wanderings, their culture and their intimate knowledge of nature.

In no country anywhere lives so heterogeneous a society or, as indicated in this chapter, such a colourful kaleidoscope of humanity.

CONSTITUTION AND GOVERNMENT SYSTEMS

Before Union in 1910 the two British Colonies and two Boer Republics each had its own governmental system. By 1872 the Cape had received responsible constitutional government but, although Natal followed much the same pattern, a similar constitution was only introduced there in 1893.

The National Convention in Durban.

41

The two Boer Republics were based on 19th century European constitutionalism and had borrowed freely from British, French and American experiences. In both, executive power was vested in a president, elected directly by the people, and an executive council. Legislative authority was vested in a unicameral *volksraad*. Political parties were virtually unknown – instead, leading political personalities commanded wide personal allegiances.

South Africa became a single constitutional entity less than a decade after the horrors of the Anglo-Boer War, which had engendered an aftermath of intense Boer-Brit enmity and bitterness.

Proposed by General J. C. Smuts and seconded by John X. Merriman in May 1908, a National Convention, representing the British Colonies and the defeated ex-Republics, was constituted to consider a basis for the unification of the whole country. Between October 12, 1908 and May 11, 1909 the convention met in Durban, Cape Town and Bloemfontein.

As a result of great statesmanship by the galaxy of talented delegates to the convention and in particular by Merriman, Smuts and M. J. Steyn, a proposed *South Africa Act* was drafted. It was presented to, and enacted by, a sympathetic British Government during 1909 and led the way to the declaration of the Union of South Africa on May 31, 1910. The basic constitution of Union has since remained almost unchanged, except for modifications

to accommodate the further historic change to Republican Government on May 31, 1961. May 31, a statutory holiday, which had previously been celebrated as Union Day, thereafter became Republic Day.

The Republic of South Africa is a sovereign, independent State consisting of four provinces: the Cape of Good Hope, the Transvaal, the Orange Free State and Natal.

The Republic also administers South West Africa as an integral part of the country. This was originally provided for under *Article 2* of the mandate granted by the League of Nations to the Union in December 1920. However, since the establishment of the United Nations the legality of the mandate has been in dispute. South Africa has been subjected to international pressure to relinquish control over the territory, which the UN has renamed Namibia. The South African Government has declared that it is its intention to give the peoples of South West Africa the opportunity of exercising their right to self-determination within the next few years.

Three Capitals

One of the expensive fruits of the give-and-take statesmanship that went into the drafting of *The South Africa Act* was the unique establishment of separate capitals in three of the four provinces. Cape Town is the legislative capital and the seat of Parliament; Pretoria the administrative capital and headquarters of the civil

26

service; and Bloemfontein the judicial capital and seat of the Appellate Division of the Supreme Court.

The State President

Executive power is vested in the State President, who is Head of State and acts on the advice of the Executive Council. He is elected for a term of seven years by an electoral college comprising both Houses of Parliament. Legislation becomes law when it receives his assent.

The Cabinet

The Executive Council, consisting of the Prime Minister and 17 other Ministers of State, constitutes the Cabinet. There are six Deputy Ministers, who are not members of the Cabinet. All Ministers and Deputy Ministers are customarily appointed from the members of the governing party and each Minister heads one or more State Department, which in turn has a permanent civil servant as Secretary.

The Legislature

Legislative power is vested in Parliament, which meets in Cape Town and comprises a House of Assembly *(Volksraad)* and a Senate.

The House of Assembly has 171 members elected by White voters at intervals of not more than five years: 165 represent constituencies in the Republic of South Africa and six are from South West Africa.

The Senate has 55 members: 45 elected by electoral colleges consisting of MPs and MPCs (Member of the Provincial Council) from the four provinces; 16 from the Transvaal, 11 from the Cape Province, 8 each from Natal and the Orange Free State and two elected from South West Africa. The other ten are nominated by the State President; two each from the provinces and South West Africa. The Senate is mainly a house of review, functionally similar in many respects to the British House of Lords.

Provincial Administration

Each of the four provinces has a legislature known as a Provincial Council. It is elected for periods not exceeding five years on the same franchise as the House of Assembly. The chief executive officer of each province is the Administrator who is appointed by the State President for five years. He and four members of each Provincial Council form an Executive Committee for the province. Provincial Councils are mainly concerned with matters such as education, hospital services, local authorities, roads, traffic and the preservation of fauna and flora.

Apartheid or Separate Development

The National Party policy, known as Separate Development, has been evolved from the concept of *apartheid*.

The underlying principle of the policy of Separate Development is that friction between peoples of such vastly different cultural backgrounds, as found in South Africa, can best be avoided by allowing each of these peoples to retain their own identity. Hence certain portions of land, traditionally occupied by the various Black nations, have been set aside for Black occupation only. These Bantu Homelands are being consolidated and

developed so that they may eventually attain political sovereignty, independent of the Republic of South Africa. The Blacks currently living in the Republic of South Africa will then enjoy full political rights within their own states. Also in terms of this policy the rest of South Africa will be governed by an all-White Parliament as well as Legislative Councils representing the Coloureds and Indians. In the White designated areas of the country the policy has been to provide alternative amenities for the different racial groups. Changes in administration, particularly since 1974, are now aimed at the elimination of many of these symbols of discrimination.

The National Party has steadily gained seats in the all-White Houses of Parliament, with its race policies and the Republican issue as the main platforms in its political armoury. Although the National Party's racial policy has helped to win electoral victories, it has also earned South Africa the enmity of most of the members of the United Nations, in particular of the Afro-Asians. The word *apartheid* has internationally become a swear word and a whipping stick, which has through the years resulted in South Africa's expulsion or exclusion from many international bodies and spheres of sport.

The Coloured Persons Representative Council

In 1951 the National Party decided to remove Coloured voters from the common voters' roll. The measure was challenged in the upper Courts and defeated. However, the Government solved this impasse by enlarging the Senate in 1955, thereby achieving the two-thirds majority required for the success of this controversial legislation.

To compensate the Coloured voters and in terms of the policy of Separate Development, a Coloured Persons Representative Council of the Republic of South Africa – the CRC – was established. It consists of 40 elected and 20 Government-nominated members of the Coloured community. The Council, subject to the Minister of Coloured Affairs, has legislative powers and its five member Executive is responsible, on behalf of the Coloured community, for the management of finance, education, welfare and pensions, local government, rural areas and settlements.

Despite the existence of the CRC, Coloured leaders continue to urge that their community, which has no homeland other than the Republic, be represented directly by Coloureds in the central Parliament.

South African Indian Council

The Indian communities in Natal, Transvaal and the Cape have 25 representatives in a statutory body, the South African Indian Council. They represent the many fields of Indian activity and the Council advises the Government on matters which affect the economic, social, cultural, educational and political interests of their communities. Although many Indian leaders work through this Council, they, too, hope that it will lead to eventual direct Parliamentary representation.

Justice

South African common law is based on Roman Dutch law, introduced to the Cape by the Dutch settlers in 1652. After the second British occupation in 1806 South African law was influenced to some extent by English law, but this influence has steadily diminished since the *Act of Union.*

Roman Dutch law has in fact been adapted over the years to suit the complex structure of the country. South African law now consists of common law, statute law and case law, the latter based on Supreme Court decisions.

Judicial authority is vested in the several Divisions of the Supreme Court, including the Court of Appeal, certain special courts, the lower Magistrate Courts, the courts of Bantu Chiefs and Headmen and of Bantu Affairs Commissioners. The South African judiciary has a long record of impartiality and independence from the legislative and executive branches of government, and the decisions of the Appellate Division are binding on all lesser courts.

White Political Parties and their Politics

Three political parties were represented when, in January 1975, President 'Jim' Fouché opened the Republic's Parliament for the last time before his retirement.

Unrepresented were two 'splinter parties', both led by breakaway ex-National Party Cabinet Ministers. One, right wing and *verkramp* (conservative or die-hard), is the Herstigte Nasionale Party (HNP) under Dr Albert Hertzog, son of the late Prime Minister General J. B .M. Hertzog. The other is *verlig* (enlightened or 'liberal') and called the Democratic Party (DP) led by Mr Theo Gerdener.

These 'splinter parties' are but early products of the state of flux and uncertainty which has been evident in the White electorate, particularly during the 1970s. Indeed, since the beginning of the 1975 parliamentary session, rumblings and differences in policy and personality in the Opposition United Party have resulted in some of its MPs and MPCs forming another break-away party, provisionally called the Reform Party which, too, is *verlig*.

Likewise, in the ruling National Party, there has been evidence of right wing dissatisfaction with the Prime Minister's policy of détente and relaxation of apartheid restrictions.

It is thus virtually impossible to present at this time a clear and detailed explanation of the actual differences in the four parties with parliamentary representation. The major differences in their respective policies do relate, however, to the peaceful solution of the multitude of racial problems which beset the country.

The National Party believes that these problems can best be solved by creating, within the Republic of South Africa's borders, independent sovereign states for the various African peoples. For the Coloured and Indian communities they regard 'the policy of parallel development with practical liaison and their own local and parliamentary institutions, alongside the White population group', as the only practical solution.

The United Party propogates a federal system of government under White leadership. The independent Black Homelands would be invited to join the broader federal system while retaining their self-governing status. The Coloured and Asiatic peoples would be afforded full citizenship and autonomy within their own communities.

The *verligte* Progressive Party, differing from the two older parties, advocates a policy of 'shared power' in which a pattern of coexistence would be worked out by White, Black, Coloured and Indian in consultation with one another. There would be a central parliament elected by voters with reasonable educational, income or property qualifications.

The *verligte* 'Reform Party' has yet to form and state its policy.

The following tables indicate the results of some of the more dramatic elections in recent decades:

	1938	1948	1961	1974
National Party	27	70	105	123
United Party	111	65	49	41
Labour Party	3	6		
Afrikaner Party		9		
Progressive Party			1	7

The future of South Africa's political parties will be greatly influenced by changing *verligte* and *verkrampte* adherences . . . and by happenings in Africa in general, and Southern Africa – including South West Africa – in particular.

GEOGRAPHY

South Africa, strategically situated at the southern tip of Africa, lies almost entirely within the southern temperate zone, between 22°S and 35°S. It is part of the great and fascinating African plateau which occupies most of the continent south of the Sahara. The plateau is for the most part formed of near-horizontal rock strata of Mesozoic and pre-Mesozoic age. In places these formations have been tilted, warped, folded and eroded, giving distinctive local variations in their physiography. Geology is varied and ranges from vast thicknesses of Karoo rock to the highly complicated rock assemblages associated with the Bushveld Igneous Complex and Archaean formations. And, associated with the latter, the oldest known rocks on earth are to be found in Swaziland.

The average elevation in most parts of South Africa is 1 200m while the country's general appearance could be described as a vast inverted dinner plate – a high escarpment rises steeply to the east and south-east, slopes gently to the west coast and encircles an enormous interior plateau.

Nature has actually divided South Africa into four regions, each with its own fascination: a narrow coastal belt between escarpment and sea at an average altitude of less then 300m; the Little Karoo, narrow, table-flat in the south and separated from the coastal plains by the Langeberg and Outeniqua mountain ranges – average elevation 460m; the Great Karoo, wide open areas, separated from the Little Karoo by the Swartberg and Suurberg ranges – undulating elevations range between 600m and 900m; and finally the vast Highveld, comprising the Northern Cape, Orange Free State and most of the Transvaal, with an elevation ranging from 1 200m to 1 800m (Johannesburg, for example, is 1 800m above sea level).

For perspective, some comparisons in the geographic situations between cities in South Africa and her two other southern hemisphere 'neighbours' are of interest. For instance, Cape Town, Buenos Aires in Argentina and Sydney in Australia are all on almost the same latitude; likewise Durban and Porto Alegre in Brazil, with Brisbane in Australia only a few degrees north.

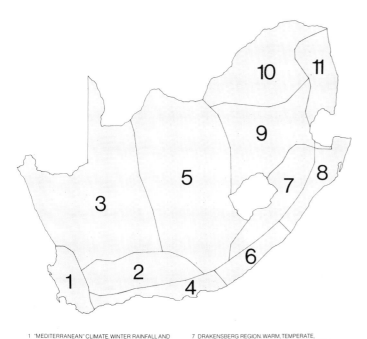

1 "MEDITERRANEAN" CLIMATE. WINTER RAINFALL AND DRY SUMMERS.
2 GREAT AND LITTLE KAROO. TRANSITIONAL ZONE FROM WINTER TO SUMMER RAINFALL.
3 DESERT CLIMATE. RAINFALL LOW AND UNRELIABLE.
4 TEMPERATE, WARM AND HUMID. RAIN ALL SEASONS.
5 SEMI-ARID. SUMMER RAINFALL. LARGE SEASONAL RANGE OF TEMPERATURE.
6 WARM, TEMPERATE AND HUMID. SUMMER RAINFALL.
7 DRAKENSBERG REGION. WARM, TEMPERATE, MONSOONAL CLIMATE. SUMMER RAINFALL. WINTER SNOW (SOMETIMES).
8 WARM AND HUMID. SUMMER RAINFALL.
9 HIGHVELD. WARM, TEMPERATE, MONSOONAL CLIMATE. SUMMER RAINFALL AND DRY WINTERS.
10 SUB-TROPICAL. SEMI-ARID. SUMMER RAINFALL.
11 SUB-TROPICAL LOWVELD. WARM AND OPPRESSIVE EXCEPT IN MID-WINTER.

Climatic Regions.

CLIMATE

South Africa offers climatic conditions for men of all seasons and seasons for all men.

For example, Cape Town is wet and cold in winter – June, July and August – but is mild, warm and Mediterranean-like, in spring, summer and autumn respectively. Johannesburg, in contrast, is dry and hot with rain in summer, but has invigoratingly crisp dry days and cold, sometimes freezing, nights in winter. Durban has very hot, humid and wet summers but pleasant and comfortably mild winters.

This enormous range of climatic conditions in South Africa is due in part to the vastness of the country and to the great variety of relief and geography. The weather and climates are also strongly influenced by the position of the subcontinent in relation to the pressure and wind systems generated by the surrounding cold Atlantic and warm Indian Ocean currents.

Most of the country receives summer rains. Only a comparatively small area on the south-western coast has winter rainfall, while a portion of the southern coastal strip has rain during all seasons.

The westward flow of moisture-laden winds from the Indian Ocean is significant in influencing precipitation over the eastern half of the country and, in general, rainfall decreases from east to west – from over 1 000 mm a year along the east coast to less than 125 mm in the Namib and Namaqualand desert areas in the west. The altitude of the escarpment areas and mountain ranges also causes greater rainfall near the coast and to the east of the country. On the whole about a quarter of the country receives more than 625 mm per annum, but drought conditions do occur periodically – as do floods.

Winter rains are usually soft and steady, but the sudden summer-afternoon downpours in the interior are often accompanied by violent thunder and lightning storms. Hail, too, is not uncommon in some areas.

The average number of hours of sunshine per day varies from 7,5 to 9,5 compared with 3,8 in London and 6,9 in New York. In the interior the sun shines throughout the winter months. During summer the eastern coastal belt is hot and humid due to higher rainfall, low elevation and the warm Mozambique Current. This area, with Durban as its centre, is South Africa's winter playground.

Summer temperatures on the Highveld (interior) are generally modified by altitude. For the same reason winter temperatures often drop below zero celsius at night, frost is common, but snow unusual. However, the Drakensberg in Natal, other high mountain peaks of the escarpment and some coastal mountain ranges in the Cape are at times covered in winter snow.

FAUNA

South Africa supports what has been described as the 'greatest wild-life show on earth'.

In spite of the wasteful and often cruel 'overkill' during previous centuries, large remnants of indigenous game species have survived. They have been protected by law for many recent decades. In fact, in South Africa's eight national parks and scores of reserves, the game is today so prolific that sometimes culling has to take place to save certain species from destroying their own habitat. In the process, the meat thus produced is once again becoming a significant factor in the diets of the mainly Black citizens in these areas.

The Kruger Park sanctuary (19 000km²) in the Transvaal is one of the largest and best-stocked game parks in the world. It draws thousands of tourists from every corner of the Republic and overseas to its animal-filled veld which teems with antelope, giraffe, zebra, buffalo and brilliant bird-life; with great pachyderms (elephants, hippopotamus and rhinoceros); and predators (lion, cheetah, leopard, hyena, jackal, wild dogs, etc.). Here animals enjoy the best of all worlds, living in their natural habitat as nature designed it without fear of attack and able to study at close quarters the human species in their noxious vehicles.

FLORA AND VEGETATION

South Africa has vast wealth in most natural resources, but it is poorly endowed with indigenous forest. This is due partly to adverse climatic conditions but more to the ravages of flame and man. Experts believe that five centuries ago dense forests covered a 'timber belt' running all the way from the Soutpansberg in the Northern Transvaal, along the Drakensberg, through the Natal Midlands and down from the Transkei to False Bay in the Cape. But fires devastated large areas, African tribes cleared countless hectares for firewood and for two centuries White pioneers axed their way through the Cape forests. They required wood for houses, wagons, furniture and farm tools, but did nothing about regeneration. As a result, some of the rare woods thus used, such as Yellowwood, Black Stinkwood, Assegai Wood, Black Ironwood, to name but a few, are now being protected by the Department of Forestry to avoid their entire extinction.

Today only about 0,2% of the total land area in the Republic is covered by indigenous forest and most of this is State property. These forests are found mainly in patches along the southern and eastern coastal regions which have a regular rainfall exceeding 1 000 mm.

The Republic of South Africa is, however, wonderfully endowed in its wealth of flora. Botanist-explorers have catalogued 18 000 plant species compared with 15 000 in the USA. Even Russia, in its vast one-seventh of the Earth's land, has only a few more species than South Africa.

In the beautiful Cape Peninsula, home also of the world famous National Botanic Gardens of South Africa (Kirstenbosch), 160 hectares in extent, at the foot of Table Mountain, there are more varieties of wild plants than in the entire British Isles.

Nature reserves and botanic gardens are to be found in most cities and in many towns and villages throughout the country. Most wild flowers are protected by law and South Africans generally are proud of this great heritage and careful to preserve it.

One of the great phenomena, which attracts residents and tourists from far and wide, is the incredible show of flowers which literally erupts over thousands of square kilometres every spring, particularly after a rainy winter. And nowhere is this more dramatic or incredibly beautiful than the vast areas in the north-western Cape and Namaqualand, where the veld during frequent dry years is arid, dusty and growth-stunted.

AGRICULTURE AND FISHING

The original South African settlement in the fertile western Cape Province was founded on an agricultural and pastoral basis. But much of the Republic is arid, stony or mountainous and, while about five-sixths of its 122,3 million hectares is available for farming, a mere 10% (10,2 million hectares) of this is cultivated – including 800 000 hectares under irrigation on which crops such as lucerne, wheat, vegetables and fruit are grown.

Most of South Africa's agriculture is therefore based on dry farming. Grazing for the production of sheep and cattle and the cultivation of maize and wheat depend almost entirely on seasonal rains. Unfortunately farmers are fairly frequently victims of the vagaries of the weather – devastating droughts or raging floods – which in turn affect the country's food supplies and exports.

Many water schemes, some enormous and brilliantly conceived, are under construction in all the provinces. The most ambitious among these is the Orange River Development Project commenced in 1963. It will be the largest water-supply scheme in Africa and when completed will irrigate 294 000 hectares and supply, initially, 454 600 m³ of water a day for domestic and industrial purposes. Two hydroelectric generators with a rated capacity of 80 MW each have been constructed at the massive Hendrik Verwoerd Dam, which is a spectacular part of this sprawling complex of dams, canals and underground tunnels.

Despite the limitations imposed by soil conditions, climate and topography, South Africa produces a large variety of livestock, crops, fruits and vegetables. With but a few exceptions the country is virtually self-sufficient in food, yet still able to earn vast amounts of foreign exchange from exports of maize, wool, fruit, fish, wine and other products. The gross value of agricultural production increased from R444 million in 1949/50 to R1 629 million in 1972/73.

Maize (Corn): Maize is the Republic's most important single crop and South Africa is a net exporter of this staple commodity so vitally needed in many food-hungry countries. The 1972/73 season produced 4 247 973 metric tons valued at over R355 million.

Wheat: Although wheat is produced in quantity, in the Western Cape in particular, it is not sufficient to supply the country's needs. Wheat has therefore to be imported.

Sugar: Sugar-cane is grown along the Natal coast belt, in areas of the Natal Midlands, in Zululand and in the Eastern Transvaal. Production totalled 1,8 million metric tons in 1973 of which about half was exported. Earnings from exports in 1973 amounted to R105 million.

Tobacco: The gross value of tobacco produced in 1972/73 was R26,6 million of which surpluses to local requirements are exported. Virginian kiln-dried and air-dried tobacco, the main growth, is produced in the Transvaal, while Turkish tobacco comes mainly from the Western Cape.

Fruit: South Africa produces a great variety of fruits with an annual gross value of about R100 million.

Deciduous fruits, especially apples, apricots, peaches, pears, plums and grapes are grown mainly in the Western Cape. Fresh and canned products including jams and juices are exported. So, too, are dried and fresh fruits. Pineapples both fresh and canned are produced and exported from the Eastern Cape.

Citrus is grown in various parts of the country and about 54% is exported as fresh fruit. Foreign currency earned from deciduous and citrus fruit in 1973 totalled R89,2 million of which a large percentage came from Britain, where South African fruits have been popular for many decades.

Wine: Wine has been produced at the Cape since the time of van Riebeeck. Five thousand farmers, cultivating approximately 230 million vines on some 323 750 hectares, produced 531 million litres of wine and wine spirit (alcohol) in 1972. South Africa ranks 12th among wine-producing countries in the world. Her red wines in particular compare very favourably with their European counterparts and her dessert wines, sherries and brandies are in great demand overseas, especially in Great Britain and Scandinavia.

Cattle: Excluding the Black Homelands, it was estimated in May 1973 that South Africa's livestock population included 8,2 million head of cattle and 29,3 million sheep. The gross value of dairy products is some R150 million annually and in 1972 red meat production totalled 411 000 tons.

South Africa is the fifth largest wool producer in the world and its 1972 clip was valued at R142 million, of which approximately 95% was exported.

Fishing: Since World War II the fishing industry has developed so enormously that South Africa, with South West Africa, now ranks sixth in the world among fish producers and second after Peru for fish-meal.

Delectable Cape rock-lobsters caught along the west coast between Cape Town and Walvis Bay are in great local and overseas demand. Eighty percent of the 1973 catch, valued at R16 million, was exported to Europe and the USA frozen whole, as frozen tails, canned or live.

MINERAL RESOURCES

A catalogue of South Africa's mineral treasures reads like pages out of Ripley's *Believe It or Not* records. More than 50 minerals are mined and in these terms it is one of the richest countries in the world. Nearly 700 000 people are employed in mining, the country's biggest industry and main provider of foreign exchange.

Precious Metals

Gold: Since its discovery nearly 100 years ago, this metal has been South Africa's most important export. Today a honeycomb of mines, some more than a mile below ground, produces 77% of the gold of the Free World (Canada the second largest producer accounts for about 7%). In 1974 production was a colossal 758 505 kg which realised over R2 000 million. Because of the meteoric rise in the value of gold, the combined working profit of the mines was five times higher in 1974 than in 1971.

Platinum: This metal was originally discovered in 1923 in the Waterberg district of the Northern Transvaal. Since then many other outcrops and reef areas have been discovered and are being mined. South Africa's production is presently second only to Russia, and a new mine, which came into production recently, should make her the world's largest platinum producer.

Diamonds: First discovered in 1866, South Africa today produces more gem-quality diamonds than any other country. These are found in unique volcanic pipes of blue earth and in vast alluvial deposits, particularly at the mouth of the Orange River. Here bulldozers strip the dunes to expose the diamonds below and huge dikes and paddocks permit the recovery of gems from the ocean bed. In 1973, production of 7 278 000 carats earned R154 996 000.

Base Minerals

Coal: Coal-mining commenced 120 years ago. By 1973, 62 mines in the Transvaal, Orange Free State and Natal had sold a total 60,2 million metric tons, value R126 800 000. Proved and known reserves are estimated at 24 000 million tons, with a further potential reserve of about an equal amount. Coal is South Africa's major source of energy. By the mid-1980s coal will also be a large earner of foreign currency and South Africa is expected to be the largest exporter of thermal coal in the world.

Copper: Although copper was already known to various tribal peoples when the early settlers first arrived at the Cape – Governor Simon van der Stel sought the metal in the wastes of Namaqualand 300 years ago – it has been mined in vast tonnages only

during the last quarter century. Production reached 176 000 tons by 1973 of which 132 000 tons valued at R125,3 million were exported.

Iron: The annual growth-rate of iron-ore production has been 10% over the past ten years with 14 producers accounting for 11 million tons during 1973. Dominating production is the giant South African Iron and Steel Industrial Corporation, Limited (ISCOR) which produces more than half of the country's steel requirements. Total ore reserves are enormous; those at Sishen in the Cape Province alone are conservatively estimated at 4 000 million tons. A giant project to link the open-cast Sishen mine with the port of Saldanha Bay will become the basis of a massive export industry with industrialised countries like Japan.

Manganese: A total of 4,25 million tons was produced in 1972 of which 3,5 million tons were exported. Reserves are over 7 000 million tons which account for 41% of the known world total.

Vermiculite: The USA and South Africa are responsible for more than 90% of the Free World's output, the Republic's share being about 33%. In 1973 156 000 tons were produced of which 137 000 tons were exported.

Asbestos: South Africa produces 8% of the world's asbestos, ranking third after Canada and Russia which produce 80% between them. Revenue from sales totals R38 million per year.

Chrome: South Africa possesses the largest reserves of chromite (chrome ore) in the Western World. They are estimated in excess of 2 000 million tons or about 75% of the Free World's reserves.

Uranium: South Africa is one of the world's main producers of uranium, mined as a by-product of gold. Research is being promoted by the Nuclear Fuels Corporation of South Africa (NUFCOR), the Atomic Energy Board and the Chamber of Mines. In April 1975 it was announced that a full-scale uranium enrichment plant is scheduled to come into operation by 1984. It is amazing to consider that this staggeringly expensive project, even following on a South African technological breakthrough which cut production costs enormously, will be totally financed by South Africa.

Other Minerals: Dozens of other minerals are mined: from antimony to vanadium and zinc.

Semi-Precious Stones: These are found in abundance. Emerald crystals account for about 75% of sales with tiger's-eye as the second biggest money-spinner. Other semi-precious stones include agate, amethyst, jade, jasper, rose quartz and verdite.

And, as if South Africa's Aladdin's Cave is not already richly enough endowed, as of 1975 it has been established that an underground treasure-house exists in the arid Bushmanland of the north-west Cape which may be the richest of any in the country – including the already fabulous goldfields.

During recent years local and overseas corporations have spent some R8 million and, with the use of sophisticated prospecting aids and photographs taken by ERTS – the Earth Resources Technology Satellite – since 1972 have verified the widespread existence in this area of copper, lead, zinc, iron, manganese, silver, titanium, diamonds, semi-precious stones and many less-known minerals. This new 'treasure house' will be able to use water from the Orange River Schemes and another Witwatersrand may well develop here in the decades ahead.

COMMERCE AND INDUSTRY

As an industrialised country South Africa cannot isolate herself from international trends or climates of uncertainty. However, she has certain major and positive factors which protect her from violent fluctuations and recessions. In the relatively stable labour situation, strikes are comparatively rare and unemployment minimal. In 1973 Gross Domestic Product (GDP) and Gross National Product (GNP) rose by over 8% and 4% respectively. Although this growth may not again be equalled for some time because of the oil-crises-triggered worldwide recession, the Government is optimistic that the Republic of South Africa can weather any storm far more easily than most developed and under-developed countries. The main contributing factors in South Africa's favour are the spectacular increases in gold and other base mineral prices and the fact that only 15% of her energy requirements depend on imported oil.

Whereas South Africa subsisted mainly on an agricultural economy until 100 years ago, she is today a major industrial power in Africa; producing and consuming more steel and electricity, for example, than all the 47 other African countries together.

The manufacturing industry contributes approximately 25% of the GDP – double the 12% derived from mining and more than double the 10% from agriculture. Almost all minerals and basic raw materials, with the exception of oil, are to be found in South Africa. This, together with factors such as the relatively low cost of fuel and power, the low taxation and modern communication systems, contributes towards the country's progress and prosperity.

Electric Power: The State-operated South African Electricity Supply Commission (ESCOM) produces about 57% of the electricity generated on the African continent. It is also relatively cheap: 0,5565 cents per unit, compared with 0,58 cents in Canada and 1,04 cents in the United Kingdom.

ESCOM, to keep abreast with economic expansion, has programmed a doubling of its present capacity of about 7 500 MW every decade.

Electricity grids already feed vast developed areas and an inter-state grid system will receive from and take power to the whole of Southern Africa. It is planned initially to buy 600 MW from the giant Cabora Bassa project in Mozambique. In addition, the country's first nuclear power station, situated north of Cape Town, is planned for operation in 1978. It is also envisaged that neighbouring Lesotho, Swaziland and South West Africa will benefit from the grid network.

Phosphates: Before the Phosphate Development Corporation (FOSCOR) commenced production at Phalaborwa, South Africa was almost entirely dependent on imported raw phosphates. FOSCOR now supplies the entire demand.

Chemicals: The chemical industry with an annual turnover in excess of R500 million is the fourth largest secondary industrial sector. Fertilisers are produced in vast quantities and all heavy chemicals the country requires should be obtainable locally before 1980.

Synthetic rubber, plastics, styrene, fibres and nylon are produced in five new chemical plants.

Engineering Industries: Metal manufacturing and engineering industries contribute 9% of the gross manufacturing output of more than R6 400 million. R520 million plus is invested in about 120 factories manufacturing farming implements and accessories – a percentage of these is exported to 40 different countries.

Three producers supply all the Republic's rolling stock needs – including passenger coaches, goods wagons and about 6 000 electric railway units annually.

Motor Industry: Approximately 15 000 motor vehicles are produced monthly in 17 assembly plants where about 55% of the materials required are locally manufactured. Automobile components are exported to over 60 countries. Over 45% of the automobiles in Africa are registered in the Republic of South Africa.

Oil-from-Coal: South Africa has no oil or natural gas fields, but is spending many millions of Rands annually on inland and off-shore prospecting and drilling. She does, however, have the South African Coal, Oil and Gas Corporation (SASOL) which is the largest economically viable oil-from-coal plant in the world.

In addition to petrol, diesel oil and industrial gas, a large variety of petro-chemical products and raw materials are produced by SASOL. In fact, before the oil price increases of 1974, SASOL was already saving the country R50 million a year in foreign exchange.

Two modern oil refineries representing total investments of R54 million are sited in Durban and Cape Town. In addition, in 1971, the National Petroleum Refinery (NATREF), a joint enterprise of SASOL, the French company TOTAL and the National Iranian Company, was erected at Sasolburg in the Orange Free State at a total cost of R70 million.

Aircraft: In 1968 the first South African-assembled jet aircraft was completed in a factory near Johannesburg. This R40 million complex is the nucleus of South Africa's growing aircraft industry.

Iron and Steel: Thanks to South Africa's enormous reserves of iron ore, she produces three times as much steel as the rest of Africa. Since going into production in 1934 the South African Iron and Steel Industrial Corporation (ISCOR) has produced more than 48 million metric tons of steel. In fact, since 1960, ISCOR has been engaged in a continuous extension programme in three plants in order to keep up with ever increasing demand and South African steel prices are among the lowest in the world.

In South Africa today the hum of modern industry is as characteristic of the country as was the throb of the African drum in days gone by.

Cape Province

Perhaps the most striking feature of the Cape Province is its great contrast in scenery and people: the beautiful Mediterranean-like Cape Peninsula, at the foot of great mountains where the first White men settled, and the vast arid Karoo; the red and brown sands of the Kalahari desert and the green fertile south-west Cape; the vine-covered slopes and wheat fields of the Western Cape and the rolling grasslands of the Transkei.

In this vast area live people of many colours, cultures and religions – Afrikaner, Xhosa, English, Coloured, Cape Malay and many others, including a tiny fragment of Stone-Age Bushmen. From the industrialist to the labourer, from the miner to the farmer, from the housewife to the nomad – all are part of this dynamic and vital society.

The Cape Province is larger than most sovereign countries – nearly three times the size of Great Britain – and constitutes approximately 59% of the surface area of the Republic. But its population is only 31,5% of that of the entire country; nearly one quarter live in the Cape Peninsula, while the east coast is also relatively well-populated. Overall population density of the Cape Province is, however, a mere six per square kilometre.

The Cape coastline measures an astonishing 1 460 km. The stark and dangerously rocky west coast is washed by the cold Atlantic, and the south and east coast by the warm Indian Ocean. These mighty seas meet in the area between Cape Point, the dramatic tip of the Cape Peninsula, and Cape Agulhas, Africa's most southerly landmark.

42

42 In 1580, when Sir Francis Drake rounded the Cape of Good Hope, the tip of the Cape Peninsula (top left), he recorded in his diary: 'This Cape is the most stately thing and the fairest cape we saw in the whole circumference of the earth.'

43

44

45

46

43 From Bloubergstrand, the lights of Cape Town grace the foot of Table Mountain. **44** View across Table Bay. **45** The winter North-Wester brings rain and heavy seas into Table Bay roadstead. **46** Part of the city centre, much of it built on land reclaimed from the sea during harbour development.

47

48

47 Looking across Table Bay from Signal Hill. The municipal area of Cape Town is 266 km² but extends in name over a far larger area. In 1970 it had a population of 1 096 500. **48** An open-air art exhibition in a traffic-free mall. **49** Hang-gliding from the Tygerberg Hills, Parow. **50** The Houses of Parliament, officially opened in May 1885. **51** The Kat, facing the central square of the Castle which was built under Dutch rule in 1665, now houses part of

49

50

51

52

53

54

the William Fehr Collection of South African historic art. **52** A squirrel in the Public Gardens, originally developed by the Dutch East India Company to provide fresh produce for passing ships. **53** Morning fog over central Cape Town. **54** Longmarket Street. On 17th century maps this street is shown as a nameless track but, as it skirts Greenmarket Square, it received the name 'Langemarkt Straat' in 1790.

55 Bus stop. **56** The Grand Parade, established in 1697 as a military parade-ground, with the City Hall and Table Mountain in the background. On Wednesday and Saturday mornings it is a bustling flea-market. **57** A bleak winter's day. **58** Shortmarket Street, originally called 'Thuynstraat' (Garden Street) because of the vegetable gardens of burghers living nearby. **59** The flower market in central Cape Town is renowned for its

59

60

61

62

flamboyant characters, who give customers their moneysworth in provocative conversation as well as flowers. **60** Koopmans De Wet house, Strand Street, was built in 1701. Twice enlarged during that century it is a prime example of late 18th century Cape Dutch architecture and a national monument. **61** Old bottles, today valued as collectors' items, for sale on the Grand Parade. **62** Flower seller.

63

64

65

66

67

68

63 Work break. **64** Pavement games, played daily during the lunch hour, draw many onlookers. **65** Barefoot newspaper-sellers, each with his own exclusive beat, brave both the traffic and the elements. **66** The Lutheran Church complex, Strand Street, was erected by a wealthy merchant, Martin Melck, in 1774 as a 'storeroom'. In those days only the Dutch Reformed Church was tolerated at the Cape. **67** The Old Town House in Greenmarket Square houses the Michaelis Collection of paintings. **68** Greenmarket Square dates back to 1696 and derives its name from the time when it was a vegetable market.

70

71

72

73

74

75

69 Part of the small-boat harbour in Cape Town docks, with a modern stern-trawler on the right. Over two million tons of fish are caught annually in South African waters. **70** The Royal Cape Yacht Club's basin overflowing with Cape to Rio contestants. This triennial event is part of the international racing calendar. **71** Planing before a stiff South-Easter shortly after the start of the 1973 Cape to Rio yacht race. **72** Extras racing in Table Bay waters better-suited to sea-going keel yachts. **73** National Yachting Championships in False Bay. **74** During 1974 over 4 350 ships docked at Cape Town, second largest port in South Africa after Durban. **75** Model aircraft championships.

76 Part of Cape Town's freeway system. 77 Evening traffic. 78 Because South Africa is blessed with an abundance of coal, dwindling numbers of steam locomotives are still in use and attract enthusiasts from all over the world. 79 Derelict houses on the slopes of Signal Hill. Many of the cottages in this area have been charmingly renovated. 80 An old part of District Six,

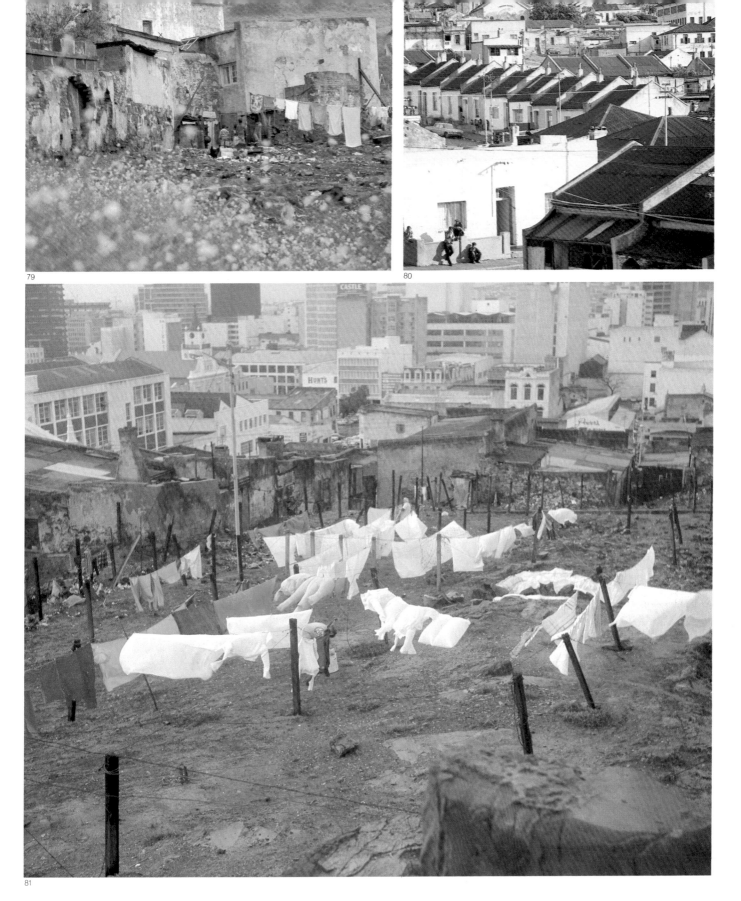

79

80

81

a residential area with a long and varied history. It is fast changing its picturesque character in the face of modern development. **81** In the Malay Quarter above the city, on the slopes of Signal Hill, washing hangs out to dry. There are less than 150 000 Malays in the Republic, almost all of whom live in the Cape Peninsula.

83

84

85

86

87

88

89

82 The Zinatul Islam Mosque in District Six. **83** Restored Malay cottages. **84** In Plein Street, one of the last old buildings doomed to make way for a city tower block. **85** The Coon Carnival, a traditional Cape Coloured festival held on the second day of the New Year. **86** Foyer of the Nico Malan Opera House. **87** Go-go dancer in a Cape Town night club. **88** A hotel, flats and shops – these multi-storied buildings are part of the changing suburban way of life. **89** Capetonians helplessly battle the South-Easter. This wind sometimes blows at gale force and keeps the city relatively smog-free during the summer months – hence its nickname 'The Cape Doctor'.

90 The 1975 Multi-National Athletics Championships held at Green Point Stadium. **91** Form of a different sort at the Kenilworth Racecourse. **92** A Sunday picnic in the Tokai Forest. **93** Morning suits and bowlers at Kenilworth Racecourse. **94** Groote Schuur Hospital, the teaching hospital of the University of Cape Town Medical School. It became world famous

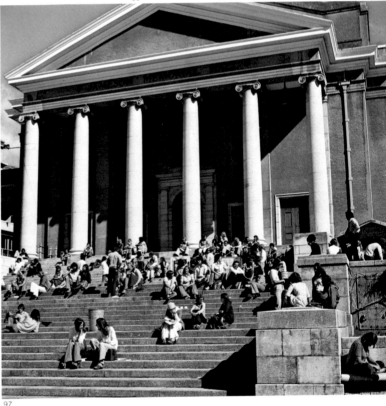

when the first heart transplant was carried out here in 1967. **95** Only minutes from the city centre spring flowers bloom on Signal Hill. **96** The University of Cape Town, oldest in South Africa, has an enrolment of 8 000 students and one of the most beautiful campuses in the world. **97** A favourite student haunt, the steps of Jameson Hall on the university campus.

98

99

100

98 Part of the Marina da Gama village complex near Muizenberg.
99 100 Restored Cape cottages at Newlands. **101** Marina da Gama – here residents can boat close to their doorstep. **102** The Tokai Manor House built in 1792 is a fine example of Cape Dutch architecture.

103

104

105

106

107

103 Saturday morning school-rugby. **104** The Cape Hunt – a halt in the Tokai Forest. **105** Historic Steenberg House, Tokai, has the only holbol (concavo-convex) gable in the Cape Peninsula. **106** Garden-party gossip. **107** Constantia, an elegant residential suburb some 20 minutes from the city centre.

108

109

110

111

112

113

114

108 Squatters on the sandy False Bay area of the Cape Flats. Despite an extensive housing programme the authorities have been unable to cope with the Coloured population explosion – between 1960 and 1970 numbers have increased by more than 30%. **109** Typical interior of a Cape Dutch house. **110** Residential area of Zeekoevlei. **111** *Protea cynaroides*, giant or king protea, national flower of South Africa. **112** Pypie *(Gladiolus maculatus* ssp. *meridionalis.)* **113** *Erica vestita,* trembling heath. **114** *Erica cerinthoides,* red erica.

115

116

117

115 Winter wandering on a lonely Cape beach. **116** Tanker rounding Cape Point. A helicopter service ferries fresh provisions and changes of crew to supertankers using the Cape route. Cape Town is one of the few ports on the African coast providing major repair facilities. **117** Collecting 'sea-

treasures' along the False Bay coast. **118** The elation of pure white sand and translucent sea. **119** Sunset over the Atlantic. **120** One of the four sheltered beaches at Clifton, renowned for its pretty girls. **121** Injured sailor brought ashore by helicopter off Cape Point.

122

123

124

125

126

122 Gordon's Bay, on the False Bay coast, nestles below the Hottentots Holland Mountains and Sir Lowry's Pass. 123 View of Camps Bay and the Twelve Apostles mountain range. 124 Flats and houses cling to Bantry Bay's narrow rocky coast making rooftop parking at street-level a common sight. 125 Baboon suckling her young on Chapman's Peak Drive. 126 Flamingoes feed at Rondevlei Bird Sanctuary on the Cape Flats.

127

128

129

127 Netting harders – a type of mullet common in Cape waters. **128** Hout Bay and Chapman's Peak. **129** A beach between Gordon's Bay and Pringle Bay on the False Bay coast. **130** The Cape roller, internationally known among surfing enthusiasts. **131** Chapman's Peak, overlooking the sea south of Hout Bay, was formerly known to English sailors as Chapman's

Chance. The Chapman's Peak Drive, famous for its spectacular views, winds high above the sea, hugging the precipitous cliff-face. Built between 1915 and 1922, it remains an impressive engineering achievement. **132** Fishing harbour at Hout Bay, a deep inlet on the west coast of the Cape Peninsula.

133

134

135

136

133 *Phylica plumosa,* commonly known as 'veerkoppie' (featherhead), in Helderberg Nature Reserve near Somerset West. **134** Owing to the difference in water temperature, many fish species in False Bay are not found in Table Bay – although they are separated by only a few kilometres of land. **135** *Helichrysum lancifolium,* a dwarf everlasting which grows in rock crevices at the summit of the Langeberg, Swellendam. **136** Hermanus, 120 km south-east of Cape Town, is a popular holiday resort and one of the finest rock-fishing areas in the world. **137** Farmhouse near Swellendam in the south-west Cape. Swellendam, established in 1747, is the third oldest town in South Africa. It has several famous historical monuments including the oldest existing Drostdy (residence and office of the landdrost or magistrate).

137

138

139

140

138 Cape sugarbird *(Promerops cafer)*. **139** Egyptian goose *(Alopochen aegyptiacus)*. **140** Bontebok *(Damaliscus dorcas dorcas)* at the Bontebok National Park near Swellendam. **141** Nesting Cape weavers *(Ploceus capensis)*. No fewer than 843 species of bird have been recorded in Southern Africa compared with 453 in Western Europe.

141

142

142 The Matroosberg (2 251 m), highest peak in the Western Cape, under snow. **143** Wheat fields near Riviersonderend. Prior to 1968 wheat was imported to South Africa. However, record crops since then have made the country self-sufficient. **144** Farm near Robertson with the imposing Langeberg Range in the background. This region produces 22% of South Africa's wine. **145** Jonkershoek Forest Reserve near Stellenbosch is used primarily for research into indigenous vegetation and means of combating fires. **146** A breathtaking view from the Franschhoek Pass of one of the richest fruit and vine growing areas in the Western Cape.

143

144

145

146

147

148

149

147 Wine cellar near Bonnievale, 65 km south-east of Worcester. 148 The Breede (Broad) River near Worcester was known to Portuguese seafarers and appeared on maps before 1502 as the Rio de Nazaret. 149 A forest glade in autumn. 150 Harvesting wheat in the south-western Cape. 151 *Aloe ferox* near Swellendam. Aloes are indigenous to South Africa and its neighbouring islands. Of 300 known species, 132 occur in South Africa. The leaves of *Aloe ferox* are used in the preparation of 'Cape Aloe Juice' which has been used for medicinal purposes for centuries and is still exported. 152 A popular Cape pastime.

153

154

155

153 Preparing hard cuttings for planting vines. **154** Coloured grape-picker. The South African wine industry dates back to February 2, 1659, when Jan van Riebeeck wrote in his diary: 'Today, Praise be the Lord, wine was made for the first time from Cape grapes.' When the French Huguenots arrived at the Cape in 1688 the quality of wine-making improved rapidly. **155** Coloured workers among the vines. **156** Auctioning cuttings of wine cultivars at Paarl. The disease *phylloxera,* which destroyed vines the world over in the 1880s, caused Cape farmers faced with bankruptcy to replant

156

with certain American varieties resistant to the disease. Today some 350 million vines flourish in the Western Cape. **157** Monument to the Afrikaans language near Paarl. **158** In order to develop the export market, co-operative wineries were established. The 'Kooperatieve Wijnbouwers Ver-eniging van Zuid-Afrika, Beperkt', (KWV), was registered at Paarl in 1918 and later became the single controlling body of the wine industry. It is the largest wine co-operative in the world. **159** Cathedral Cellar at KWV, Paarl. In 1972, over 500 million litres of wine were produced in South Africa.

160

161

160 Start of the 1974 Berg River Canoe Marathon, an annual four-stage race which covers a total distance of 166 km, from Paarl to the estuary at Velddrif. This is soon to become an international event. **161** Practising for the canoe marathon. **162** Grey herons *(Ardea cimerea),* posed like sentinels over glassy water. **163-165** Boeresport: Once a year farmers from the surrounding countryside gather at Melkbosstrand, 27 km from Cape Town, for fun and games on the beach.

162

163

164

165

166 Part of Die Braak (The Common) at Stellenbosch, with the old Kruithuis (powder-magazine) on the left. Stellenbosch was founded in 1679 by Governor Simon van der Stel, who named it after himself. It was the first village outside the Cape Peninsula. **167** Cape Dutch homestead built in 1880 on the Nederberg wine estate in the Paarl district. **168** A distant view of Table Mountain from the Simonsberg near Stellenbosch. **169** Gable of the Cape Dutch house, Blauwklippen, near Stellenbosch. **170** Student on the campus of the Afrikaans-medium University of Stellenbosch. Although the burghers at the Cape regarded Dutch as their cultural language, they spoke Afrikaans long before the end of the 18th century. Afrikaans was, however, considered by some to be the tongue of the uneducated. In 1876 the first Afrikaans newspaper, the weekly *Die Afrikaanse Patriot*, was published, but it was only in 1925 that an act of Parliament gave Afrikaans official language status.

170

171 Cottage at McGregor. 172 Cottages at picturesque Wuppertal. Until recently the Coloureds at Wuppertal produced handmade velskoene (shoes) and hand-rolled chewing tobacco under the auspices of the mission station founded by German missionaries. 173 Cape cottage. The chimney-like structure is the bakoond (baking oven) traditionally used for

175

176

177

178

baking bread. **174** Fishermen's cottages, Arniston. **175** Country cottage. **176** Cottages at Elim, a Coloured settlement and mission station. Elim boasts the oldest water-mill still grinding wheat in South Africa. **177** Cottages at Mamre, a village and mission station in the attractive rural surroundings of the Malmesbury district. **178** Cottage near Oudtshoorn.

179

180

181

179 Farm cottage in the wine district near Stellenbosch. **180** Peaches drying in the sun near Prince Alfred's Hamlet. Approximately 15 000 tons of fruit are dried each year, of which nearly 50% is exported. **181** Wheatlands near Moorreesburg, 105 km from Cape Town. **182** Tulbagh, established in

182

183

184

1795, was badly damaged by an earthquake in 1969. Church Street has been painstakingly restored and today boasts the greatest concentration of national monuments in the country. **183** Threshing wheat. **184** There are over 300 000 sheep, mostly Merino, in the Piketberg district.

185

186

187

188

185 Ursinias in the Biedouw-Valley, near Clanwilliam. Well over 18 000 different plant species have been recorded in South Africa. **186** Farmhouse, with chinkerinchees *(Ornithogalum thyrsoides)* in the foreground, near the Berg River mouth. **187** Arranging exhibits for the annual Caledon Wild Flower Show. **188** Wine cellar near Stellenbosch on the farm 'Het Verblyf der Gelukzaligen'. Vineyards are often overgrown with wild raddish during winter. **189** Wild ursinias, commonly called Namaqualand daisies, near Darling. **190** Varkslaai *(Conicosia pugioniformis)* is a common winter-flowering succulent in the Cape Sandveld. **191** Everlastings or sewejaartjies *(Helichrysum sesamoides)*. **192** Cape rain-daisies *(Dimo-*

189 193 197 201   190 194 198 202   191 195 199 203   192 196 200 204

photheca pluvialis). **193** Arum lilies *(Zantedeschia aethiopica),* common in many roadside ditches in the south-west Cape. **194** Elim heath *(Erica regia).* **195** Painted lady *(Gladiolus debilis).* **196** The pypie *(Gladiolus gracilis)* is sweetly scented and flowers in autumn and early winter. **197** Bot River protea *(Protea compacta).* **198** Pincushion *(Leucospermum guein-* *zii).* **199** The rare marsh-rose *(Orothamnus zeyheri).* **200** Sand orchid or ewatrewa *(Satyrium carneum).* **201** *Leucadendron bonum,* a rare species from the Cedarberg. **202** Kreupelhout *(Leucospermum conocarpodendron).* **203** Knoppiesbos *(Brunia nodiflora).* **204** *Gazania lichtensteinii,* one of the gousblomme of the Karoo.

205 Rainfall in Namaqualand is scant, sometimes as low as 50 mm a year. It is estimated that the area carries over half a million sheep raised for mutton. **206** The main road through Namaqualand in spring. After a wet winter, the area bursts into a multi-coloured carpet. The bright orange flowers are *Arctotis factuosa* while the copper-coloured ones are *Osteospermum pinnatum.* **207** A mixture of *Arctotis* (deep orange), *Felicia*

211

(blue), *Arcthotheca* (yellow) and *Heliophila* (blue, in the distance). The Cape Province alone has more varieties of wild plants than the entire British Isles. **208** Masses of *Grielum humifusum*. **209** Cape rain-daisies *(Dimorphotheca pluvialis)*. **210** Namaqualand ursinias bloom in spring. **211** Ursinias. Wild flowers turn to face the sun and viewers should plan their route with this in mind.

212

213

214

215

212 A tranquil section of the 'ships' graveyard' – the treacherous coastline near Agulhas. **213** Regatta at Saldanha, 90 km north of Table Bay. This large natural harbour is being developed as a port for the abundant iron-ore deposits being mined at Sishen in the North-West Cape. An 850 km railway line will connect Sishen with Saldanha – probably the longest single-

216

217

218

219

220

221

purpose line anywhere in the world. **214** West-coast fishermen.
215 Trawler off Hondeklip Bay. The fish caught are frozen at sea. **216** Near Churchhaven, a fishing village on the Saldanha Lagoon. **217** West-coast fishing trawler. The growth of the South African fishing industry in the last 30 years has been remarkable: 1 900 000 tons were processed in 1969 com-

pared with 7 500 tons in 1943. A quota system guards against over-fishing, although little can be done to prevent foreign trawlers from operating in the rich waters off South Africa. **218** Crayfish bakkies (dinghies). **219** Mending seine nets at Doring Bay. Synthetic floats have replaced cork and glass. **221** Sun-cured fish (bokkems) at Velddrif, near Saldanha Bay.

222

223

224

222 Flamingoes, south-west Cape. **223** Fishermen. **224** Cape gannets *(Morus capensis)* on Bird Island near Lambert's Bay. The young gannets migrate as far as 3 200 km along the west coast. **225** Bird Island.

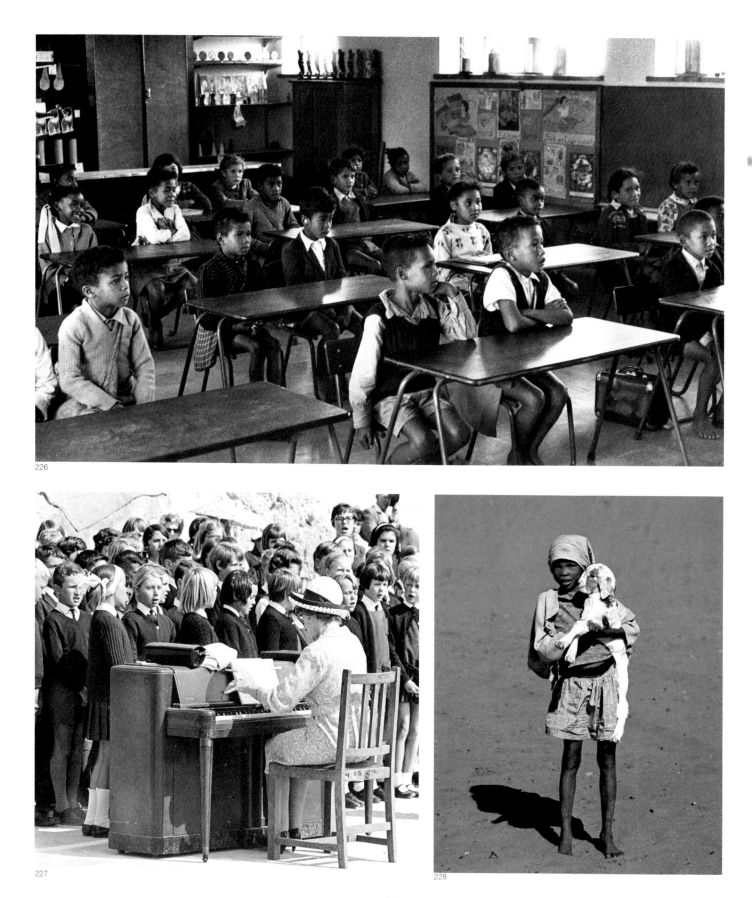

226 Classroom in a country school. **227** A school choir. **228** Hottentot girl with kid. The striking red colour of the sand is typical of the drier parts of the Kalahari, where there is insufficient water to dissolve the iron oxide which colours the grains. **229** A Bushman camp in the Kalahari. The Bushmen lead a nomadic existence, depending entirely on game and wild plants for food. When no moisture is available, they draw on seemingly invisible underground sources and the sap of various roots. Expert trackers, they can cover immense distances in search of game.

230 Windmills. Arid areas rely heavily on subterranean water sources. **231** Even donkey carts have punctures. These carts are known as 'donkie hemels' (donkey heavens) because they run on pneumatic tyres instead of the usual bone-shaking cart wheels. **232** The Augrabies Falls on the Orange River has a drop of about 150 m. The first White man to see them was a deserter from the Dutch East India Company in 1778. **233** The overall

235

236

237

238

population density of Namaqualand is one person per square kilometre.
234 At Keimoes on the banks of the Orange River. **235** Gemsbok (oryx) in
the Kalahari Gemsbok National Park – the most extensive (9 450 km²) in the
Cape Province. **236** River in the north-east Cape. **237** Quiver-tree or
kokerboom *(Aloe dichtoma)*. Bushmen used the hollowed-out branches for
holding poison arrows. **238** A country craftsman.

239

240

241

239 Typical Karoo landscape. For many South Africans who have become city dwellers, the Karoo holds a special place. The name is derived from a Hottentot word meaning 'the place of the great dryness'. It constitutes almost one third of the area of South Africa and is steadily growing. The typical Karoo vegetation, which has evolved to withstand drought, ex-

tremes of temperature and intense sunlight, is encroaching into the adjoining grassveld region. It is estimated that the eastward movement, which has been aided by destructive farming practices, has been as much as 240 km. Some traders and farmers have made their fortunes here, although the Karoo is relatively poor compared with the rest of the country. It carries

242

243

over half the sheep population of the Cape Province. Mineral wealth is limited and apart from Kimberley there is little industrial development. As a result the population has decreased by over 5% during the last ten years as compared with an increase in South Africa as a whole of more than 20%. The vastness of the area, its relative poverty and sparse population have led to the creation of remote villages often consisting of a single dusty street. **240** Palominos bred in the Richmond district. **241** General dealer — essential in a Karoo town. **242** Seventy percent of the boer goats in South Africa are owned by Blacks. These animals provide them with food and clothing and are highly valued. **243** Desolate graveyard.

244 Typical house in Graaff-Reinet. Established in 1785, Graaff-Reinet is the third oldest country town in South Africa and many of its buildings have been carefully restored. **245** Part of Victoria West, centre of a wealthy wool-producing area of the Karoo. **246** Wood-panelled door of a house in Graaff-Reinet. **247** A striking old stained-glass doorway.

248

249

250

251

252

253

254

255

256

257

258

248 Baking bread in a bakoond. **249** Karoo character. **250** One of the few remaining diamond concessions. **251** The butchery. **252** Country store. **253** An old-timer – friendlier people are difficult to find. **254** A farmhand relaxes. **255** Country garage workshop. **256** A Karoo farmer and one of his prize Merino ewes. **257** As handy as most men! **258** Few farmers still use one of these horse-drawn ploughs.

259

260

261

259 The discovery of diamonds in 1866 marked a turning-point for South Africa. From an agricultural society it became a rich industrialised nation. During the diamond rush of 1871 thousands of fortune-seekers from all over the world excavated Colesberg Kopje, which eventually became the 'Big Hole', still one of the largest manmade holes in the world. South Africa is the

262

263 264

main producer of gem-quality diamonds in the world, with 7 278 000 carats earning R154 996 000 in 1973. **260** Moonshiners busily employed near Jacobsdal. **261** On the way to the dorp (country town). **262** Deserted farmhouse in the Karoo. **263** The hotel bar at Matjiesfontein. **264** Matjiesfontein, 240 km from Cape Town, was established in 1877 by a young Scot, James Logan. It thrived as a health resort and became the headquarters of the Cape Command during the Anglo-Boer War. The entire village, consisting of less than 20 buildings, was recently restored to its former splendour and comes as a welcome surprise after a monotonous journey through the lonely Karoo landscape.

265

266

267

268

269

265 Ostrich farming near Ladismith. Commercial ostrich-farming in South Africa began in 1867. A peak was reached in 1913 when ostrich feathers were all the rage and 450 000 kg were exported. In 1914 there were 750 000 birds in South Africa, mostly in Oudtshoorn, but the ostrich boom collapsed in that same year when the era of the motor-car brought about a change in fashion. By 1940 the number of birds had dropped to 6 000. However, the market has slowly recovered, largely owing to the successful tanning of ostrich skin. **266** The Cango Caves near Oudtshoorn were discovered in 1780, reputedly by a slave. They are one of the greatest natural wonders of the world. The main chambers and passages lead to

270

271

272

others which branch in all directions, and new caverns are still being discovered. **267** Looking down from the Swartberg Pass, one of the most spectacular in South Africa. Opened in 1888 it took hundreds of convicts four years to build and rises over 1 000 m from the foot of the mountain. **268** Ostrich-riding near Oudtshoorn where a visit to one of the nearby ostrich farms is a great tourist attraction. **269** You have been warned! **270** *Aloe ferox* in the Swartberg Mountains. **271** View from the top of the Swartberg Pass – often closed in winter because of snow. This pass links Oudtshoorn with Prince Albert and has changed little since it was built. **272** Farmhouse in the eastern Cape.

273

274

275

276

277

278

273 Herold's Bay near George – a favourite holiday resort for farmers from inland districts. **274** Plettenberg Bay – a tourist mecca. **275** Knysna Lagoon with 'The Heads' in the foreground. Knysna, renowned for its boat-building and furniture-making, is also a favourite watersport and fishing resort. **276** The Tsitsikama Forest, on the coastal belt between Knysna and Humansdorp, extends for some 3 300 ha where 12 elephants still roam. The trees, especially stinkwood, are valued for timber. **277** Black-backed gulls *(Larus dominicanus),* one of the three gull species found in South Africa. **278** Robberg Nature Reserve near Plettenberg Bay.

279

280

281

279 Port Elizabeth, with a population of just under 500 000, is the fifth largest city and the third largest port in South Africa. The arrival of the 1820 British Settlers greatly influenced the city's development. Ford and General Motors' enormous motor assembly plants have made Port Elizabeth the Detroit of South Africa. **280** Motor parts factory at Uitenhage near Port Elizabeth. South Africa exports motor components to 60 countries.

281 Grahamstown owes its development and importance to the arrival of the 1820 Settlers. By 1831 it was one of South Africa's most important towns and remained so until, with the development of the diamond fields and the construction of a railway line which by-passed the town, its commercial significance dwindled. Today it is known for its numerous private and public schools, and Rhodes University. **282** Woman and child from the

282

small Fingo tribe. Children spend the first few years in very close physical contact with their mothers. The Fingo people were late-comers to the Transkei, having fled from Shaka, the Zulu king.

The Transkei has a total land area of 42 240 km² and 450 km of coastline. It is the first Black territory to become an autonomous Homeland and under Government policy it will also be first to receive sovereign independence.

The population consists of several tribes who all share a common language, Xhosa. The principal tribes are the Xhosa, Tembu and Pondo. One of the most beautiful areas in Southern Africa, with rolling hills, plains and blue mountains, it receives an average rainfall of more than 500 mm a year and has great agricultural potential. The extent of its mineral resources has not yet been fully established.

283

284

285

286

283 Xhosa women dancing at a beer drink – a great occasion for celebration, dancing and meeting people. They are wearing the typical Xhosa woman's headdress. **284** Pondo men sing at a dance. **285** Xhosa women in the Transkei. **286** Young Xhosa men in tribal finery at a dance on New Year's Day. Stick-fighting is one of the most popular activities for young men and it often occurs at social gatherings. **287** Married woman smoking a traditional pipe. **288** Young Pondo man. **289** Xhosa girls at a dance for

287

288

289

290

291

292

the unmarried. Their topless dress indicates single status. Just before marriage is a time of leisure for young people who spend much of this period attending dances and dressing up in their finery. It is the final taste of freedom before they settle down to the responsibilities of married life. **290** A beautiful bag completes this Xhosa's dance regalia. **291** Tembu youth dressed for a dance. The elaborate beadwork is often the gift of a girlfriend to her lover. **292** An initiate in the Transkei.

293

294

295

296

297

298

293 An unmarried girl. 294 A village in the Transkei with plots of maize – the staple diet of most Black people in South Africa. 295 A man's wealth is assessed by the size of his herds. Herding is the work of men and, traditionally, women were not allowed to come into contact with cattle. 296 Washday near Coffee Bay. Washing is 'beaten' clean on the flat rock surfaces. 297 A wise old man gives advice at an initiation ceremony. Great respect is shown the aged in these societies. 298 An initiate practising steps for the final circumcision ceremony, the 'umtshilo' dance. Many, but not all, Transkei tribes practise circumcision, which marks the beginning of manhood. After the circumcision has been performed by a skilled tribesman in specially constructed grass huts, the initiates, about 19 or 20 years old, live in isolation for two months or more. During this period no woman may see them. On the eighth day after the circumcision each initiate smears his body with white clay to symbolize his contact with the ancestral spirits.

Natal

When one looks at Natal's lush tones of green and brilliant colours, it is not difficult to understand why it is known as the Garden Province. Here one finds thousands of hectares of rolling fields of tall sugar-cane, exotic fruits such as paw-paws, avocado pears, mangoes, pineapples, litchis, grenadillas and, of course, bananas. Natal's 555 km long coastline is washed by the warm Indian Ocean. Its subtropical climate, the undulating Valley of a Thousand Hills and the spectacular Drakensberg mountain range make Natal South Africa's winter playground and a tourist paradise.

It is the home of over 80% of South Africa's Asians, and the imposing Zulu people, who outnumber all the Whites in the Republic, have their homeland here. It is the smallest province (a mere 7% of South Africa's land area) – yet, per square kilometre, the most densely populated.

The people of Natal are passionate horse-racing fans, and cricket is more popular here than anywhere else in the Republic. Here too, are virtually unspoilt areas for hikers, trout anglers, mountaineers and those merely wishing to relax and enjoy the sun.

299

299 Durban city centre. When Vasco da Gama sailed past the shores of Natal on Christmas Day in 1497 he gave it the name 'Terro do Natal'. Lt F.G. Farewell and Lt J. S. King produced the first chart of Port Natal (the original name for Durban) and Farewell decided to colonise the area. Finally, in 1835 the settlement that was formed was named D'Urban after the then governor of the Cape, Sir Benjamin D'Urban.

300

301

302

300 The Point Yacht Club. Durban is South Africa's principal port, an industrial centre of considerable importance, and a popular year-round holiday resort. **301** West Street, Durban. In 1845 Martin West became the first lieutenant-governor of Natal. Today West Street is the main throughfare of the city. **302** Contrast. **303** The city of Durban has a population of 843 327 (1970 Census). **304** Land-locked Durban Bay has an area of 1 668 hectares and forms a natural harbour. **305** The Golden Mile, South Beach and the Point.

303

304

305

306

307

308

309

310

311

306 Peoples and parcels travel by bus. **307** Street scene. **308** A country visitor to town. Tribal dress is unusual in most cities, but is sometimes worn on special occasions. **309** Busy shopping day. **310** An African 'muti' shop selling medicinal herbs, amulets and skins. Many African people combine Western and African beliefs; doctors, herbalists and diviners may all be consulted. **311** Snack bar. **312** Thousands of pigeons gather daily in front of the City Hall providing children with endless pleasure.

313

314

315

316

317

313 Commercial fishing along this coast is limited by the lack of exploitable shoals. **314** There are six species of whale found within a 300 km radius of Durban. Whale catches (1 850 in 1972) have been limited by International Whaling Commission quotas. **315** Durban's shipbuilding industry became firmly established in 1971 when an order was placed for two 7 300 ton vessels. It is now South Africa's shipbuilding centre. **316** A sugar terminal. Sugar is a major industry in Natal and over one million tons were exported

318

319

during 1974. These three bulk storage silos built beside the Maydon Wharf in Durban harbour have a combined capacity of 518 000 tons. **317** School children dwarfed by a mountain of sugar inside one of the storage silos. **318** Harbour tug. **319** Durban harbour, with the lights of the city in the background. The busiest port in Africa, it handled approximately 33 million tons of cargo during 1974 – more than all other South African ports combined.

320

321

322

323

324

325

320 The gaily decorated carts and brightly-feathered headgear of the 'ricksha boys' appeal to tourists. Rickshas were introduced in 1893 by a sugar magnate who imported the idea from Japan and trained sturdy Zulus to pull them. **321** An amusement centre stretches along the beachfront, often referred to as the 'Golden Mile'. **322** A wide variety of graded hotels, usually within walking distance of a beach, adds to Durban's year-round popularity. **323 324** At the 'Golden Mile'. **325** Sun, warm sand and a pillow – what more could one ask? **326** Bubbles.

326

327 The Grey Street Mosque built towards the end of the last century is the oldest in Durban. It is also one of the largest in the city centre and is surrounded by shops and flats to provide the revenue for the maintenance of the building and its associated educational and religious institutions.
328 This Hindu festival is held annually. After prayer, the participants, in a state of trance, have pins and flower-bedecked hooks inserted into their bodies. Apparently unaffected by either heat or pain, they run across a bed of red-hot coals and then proceed to a river or the sea where the pins and hooks are cast off in an act of catharsis: 'the water has washed away their sins.' **329** The fascinating Indian Market – a rich array of aromatic curries and oriental spices, souvenirs and trinkets. **330** An Imam, or prayer leader, who delivers the Friday Ghutba (sermon) and also conducts other important ceremonies. **331** Indians were indentured in 1860 to solve the sugar planters' labour problems. Soon their skills in other fields were recognised

333

and, attracted by the prospects of trade in the new colony of Natal, Gujarati-speaking traders followed. Immigration was stopped by the Indian Government in 1911 by which time 152 184 Indians had settled in South Africa. **332** Women seek bargains at the Indian Market. **333** Most Indian marriages are arranged by the parents and the ceremony provides full scope for a display of status and wealth. Nine halls in the centre of Durban have been specifically built for wedding celebrations.

334

335

336

337

338

339

334-336 Winter playground of South Africa. Over 300 000 tourists visited Durban during 1974. **337** Watching a puppet show on Durban beach. **338** Nets protect bathers from shark attack. The warm Indian Ocean and big breakers are ideal for swimming and surfing. **339** Tropical coastal waters provide excellent angling.

340

341

342

340 Members of an African Zionist church gather on the beach. In 1970 there were some 3 000 independent churches in South Africa with a membership of about 20% of the total Black population. Many of the sects can be recognised by their colourful uniforms. **341** Evangelists on Durban beach. **342** Members of an African Zionist church. Beach services are held for baptism or healing by immersion in the sea. **343** Catamarans are popular because of their ability to operate from open beaches. **344** Professional lifesavers launch a ski-boat. **345** Fishing from the pier.

343

344

345

346

347

346 347 Crowds watching rugby at the Kingsmead stadium. **348** Bowls. **349** The Durban July Handicap at Greyville, South Africa's most glamorous racing event, is run over a distance of ten and a half furlongs on the first Saturday of July each year. It attracts thousands of spectators from all over the country. **350** Preparing for a race in Durban Bay.

348

349

350

125

351

352

353

354

355

356

351 Crowds leaving Kingsmead. **352** Paw-paw trees and other tropical vegetation thrive in a climate where summers are hot and winters mild. **353** City-bound traffic on one of Durban's freeways. **354** Making glass-fibre canopies. **355** Old house in Musgrave Road. **356** Durban city centre from the residential area of Berea. **357** A chameleon – one of nine lizard families found in South Africa. Some Africans believe that the Creator sent a chameleon to promise man eternal life and a lizard to announce his mortality. Unfortunately the chameleon dawdled on the way and the lizard was the first to arrive.

357

358 Sailing at St Michaels-on-Sea on the South Coast. **359** Skin-diving is extremely popular although sharks present some danger, particularly in the summer months when water temperatures are high. **360** Pietermaritzburg City Hall, reputed to be the largest all-brick structure in the world. Pietermaritzburg, the capital of Natal, was founded by the Voortrekkers and named in honour of two Great Trek leaders, Pieter Retief and Gerrit Maritz.

361 Interior of an old church in Pietermaritzburg. **362** Street scene. **363** A cabbage plantation in fertile Natal. **364** Baskets for sale at the roadside. **365** One of Natal's oldest bookshops. The most English-speaking of the four provinces, Natal is sometimes affectionately referred to as 'the heart of the British Empire'. **366** Stone bridge in the beautifully laid-out Alexandra Park, Pietermaritzburg. This park, named after the wife of King

Edward VII, is the centre of various sporting activities. **367** Near Mooirivier, west of Durban. The bracing climate makes this area a popular health resort. **368** Valley of a Thousand Hills. Innumerable small hills surround the main valley of the winding Umgeni River and create some of the most spectacular scenery in the country. **369** Hay-making. **370** Agaves (sisal plants) against a stormy sky. The huge leaves yield an important commer-cial fibre. **371** Cattle grazing near Mooirivier. In addition to the indigenous species found in South Africa by the White settlers, various breeds have been imported from other parts of the world. Today there are more breeds in the Republic than in any other country. **372** Hilton College, 10 km from Pietermaritzburg, is a well-known private boys' school which was founded in 1868.

373 Landscape near Winterton at the foot of the Drakensberg (Mountains of the Dragon). 374 View of the Amphitheatre in the Drakensberg. This mountain range is the most important in Southern Africa, stretching for a distance of 1 046 km, roughly parallel to the eastern coastline. Near the Sani Pass between Natal and Lesotho is Thabantshonyana (3 482 m), the highest peak. To the north the mountains are less formidable, and it was here that the Voortrekkers were able to cross with their wagons into Natal. 375 Giant's Castle National Park comprises 24 121 ha of grass-covered hills and deep river valleys at the foot of the massive Drakensberg. 376 Kranskop (1 155 m). By 1970 the almost vertical faces had been scaled only three times. 377 Near Cathedral Peak. Crisp air and exquisite natural surroundings make the Drakensberg a popular holiday area for those who

380

381

382

383

want to 'get away from it all'. **378** Dirt road on a Natal farm. **379** Once a haven for the mountain Bushmen, the Drakensberg is richly endowed with examples of their art. Outstanding in design, simplicity of form and wealth of natural expression, these paintings give glimpses of their way of life and the environment in which they lived. **380** View across the Amphitheatre from the upper slopes of the Sentinel. **381** The Drakensberg follows the entire length of the eastern border of South Africa with Lesotho. Motor access is hazardous and is best tackled in a four-wheel drive vehicle. **382** The Tugela River has eroded this dramatic gorge. **383** In the Royal National Park below Mont-aux-Sources. Most of South Africa's important rivers, including the Vaal, Orange and Tugela, have their sources in or near the Drakensberg.

131

384

384 Water nymph and a cold, clear mountain stream. **385** Zulu girl fetching water. Originally a number of independent tribes, the Zulus were forged into one nation by the great Zulu kings. The Zulus are proud people, conscious of their heritage and, more than any other tribe in Southern Africa, have adhered to their customs and language. There are over four million Zulus in Natal, comprising the single largest population group in South Africa. Nearly 60% live in KwaZulu, the 3,3 million ha Zulu Homeland. **386** The practice of stretching the earlobes with wooden discs is rapidly dying out. This headdress is worn mainly by conservative traditionalists. **387** A Zulu diviner or witchdoctor.

388

389

390

391

388 A popular holiday pastime. 389 390 Covered breasts and flared headdress indicate that these women are married. 391 Unmarried girls gossip outside a trading store which is an important social centre in rural areas. 392 Trading stores supply large areas. 393 A woman, on her way to a beer drink, carries her homemade mat to sit on. She is wearing another traditional form of headdress. 394 Unmarried girl dressed for a dance.

395

396

397

398

399

400

401

402

403

404

395 The Western-influenced square shape of this hut is becoming more popular. **396** Round mud huts are less of a fire hazard and more durable than the traditional beehive shape. **397** Young girls, dressed only in bead aprons, on their way to a dance. **398 399** Pottery, an ancient Zulu craft, is traditionally done by the women. The only school of contemporary African pottery in South Africa is at Rorke's Drift. **400** Playing a homemade violin. **401** Construction of a beehive-shaped hut. The men make the flexible wattle-sapling frame while the women do the thatching. **402** Many domestic chores are performed by single girls in preparation for marriage. **403** Village headman. **404** Zulu warrior at a dance.

405 Cutting sugar-cane. The sugar industry had its beginnings in 1851 when Edmund Moorehead produced the first sugar in Natal. Today the growing of sugar-cane is Natal's main agricultural activity. Fields are sometimes set alight prior to cutting to expose the stems which contain the sugar. **406** Bamboo along the tropical North Coast. **407** Lake St Lucia was discovered in 1507 by Portuguese explorers who named it Santa Lucia. It teems with crocodile and hippo and over 350 bird species have been identified. **408** Sugarmill. Today 20 mills have a combined annual output of

411

412

413

414

415

416

two million metric tons. **409** Angling. **410** Much of Natal's rich natural forest has been cleared to make way for cane-fields. Until Union in 1910 no effective measures were taken to protect what remained. **411** Anglers are attracted by the game fish which follow the sardine run each year. **412** *Stapelia nobilis,* the giant carrion flower. **413** A paper mill. South Africa produces 80% of her paper requirements. **414** Pine forest near Amatikulu on the North Coast. **415** Selling woven mats and pots at the roadside. **416** Cane-fields.

417

418   419

417 Children warm themselves in the early morning chill. **418** Zulu elders listen to a speech. Councils of elders play an important role in traditional society. **419** The bride's retinue with the bride in its midst, arriving at a wedding. Traditionally, the marriage will only be firmly established after the birth of a child. **420** A warthog boar *(Phacochoerus aethiopicus)*. There are several game reserves along the North Coast of Natal. The best known are

Hluhluwe, Umfolozi, Mkuze and Ndumu. At times, game increases beyond the capacity of the reserves. Since 1957 the Natal Parks Board has captured game for distribution to farmers in preference to culling. **421** Herd of impala *(Aepyceros melampus)*. **422** Cheetah *(Acinonyx jubatus)*. The demand for its handsome fur and a poor breeding record in captivity have endangered the species' continued existence.

420

421

422

423

424

425

426

423 Blue wildebeest *(Connochaetes taurinus)*. Widespread throughout South Africa, large herds of blue wildebeest, or brindled gnu, are frequently found in association with zebra, springbok or impala. The lion is their main enemy. **424** Vervet monkeys *(Ceropithecus aethiops)*. **425** The white rhinoceros *(Ceratotherium simum)*, second largest of Africa's animals, was once found throughout Southern Africa. It was ruthlessly hunted for its horn, which was believed to have aphrodisiac properties, and in 1929 only some 20 remained, all in the Umfolozi Game Reserve in Zululand. Under careful protection the species is now being reintroduced to other parts of Africa. **426** Some Black peoples in South Africa regard the hammerkop *(Scopus umbretta)* with awe and will even move their huts if it flies overhead and calls.

Orange Free State

The Orange Free State is the heart of the Republic, lying between the Orange and Vaal Rivers. It consists mostly of grassy, scrub-covered plains dotted with characteristic flat-topped koppies. To the east its flatness is sharply contrasted with the striking Drakensberg mountain range. This area, with its beauty and crystal clean air, has become an increasingly popular tourist and health resort.

The climate varies between cool and invigorating winters to warm sun-filled summer days. Rainfall occurs mainly in summer, often with sudden thunderstorms.

The Free State constitutes only 10% of the land area of South Africa, and its population is a mere 7,7% of that of the Republic – but it is nevertheless both an important gold producer and a fertile agricultural region.

Freestaters can be formidable opponents on the rugby field, but are naturally warm and hospitable people. Visitors are invariably invited to join in a braaivleis (barbecue) of various meats, including the spicy South African boerewors (sausage).

427 The sunflower *(Helianthus annuus)* is widely grown for its oil which is used mainly for cooking and in paint manufacture.

428

429

430

428 Polo was introduced to South Africa in the early 1870s by British regiments serving in the country. **429** Bloemfontein is the capital of the Orange Free State and judicial capital of South Africa. Until 1848 the Voortrekkers had considered Winburg the seat of government, but when the British annexed the Free State in that year, Bloemfontein became the seat of the new administration. **430** Welkom was laid out as a garden city in 1947 and rapidly overtook Bloemfontein to become the biggest town in the

431

432

433

Free State – largely because of the rapidly expanding goldmining industry.
431 Ideal thermal conditions for all types of air sport occur over the vast
Free State plains. **432** Ladybrand, 15 km north of Maseru, capital of
Lesotho, was established in 1867. It was named after the wife of Sir
Christoffel Brand, first Speaker of the Legislative Assembly at the Cape.
433 Ficksburg was established in 1867 to defend against Basuto invaders.
It has a grand view of the frequently snow-capped Maluti Mountains.

434

435

436

434 The Orange River Project, which was started in 1963, is now well advanced and when completed will be the largest scheme of its kind in Africa. Its purpose is to provide an adequate and reliable water supply in a country where rainfall is unpredictable and droughts not uncommon.
435 The Vaal River in flood. This river, which forms the border between the Orange Free State and the Transvaal, is a tributary of the Orange River. Although it is longer and drains a much larger catchment area than the main

437

438

439

440

441

Orange headstream, it contributes less than half of the combined volume. **436** Two hydro-electric generating sets, with a rated capacity of 80 MW each, have been installed at the Hendrik Verwoerd Dam and feed a 1 600 km transmission grid which runs from the Witwatersrand to Cape Town. **437** The 948 m wall of the Hendrik Verwoerd Dam, under construction. The dam was completed in 1972. **438** Thermal power, based on the vast deposits of easily accessible coal, is the main source of electricity in the

Republic. More than 50% of Africa's electric power is generated in South Africa. **439** The Orange Free State goldfields produce 28% of the Free World's gold – by far the largest percentage of the seven South African goldfields. **440** Basuto 'boss boy' and miners at the President Brand Mine. **441** Sasolburg by night. SASOL (South African Coal, Oil and Gas Corporation Ltd) is the only concern of any consequence in the world that produces oil from coal.

442

443

444

442 View of Thaba Nchu (Black Mountain) from the main road between Bloemfontein and Ladybrand. **443** The Dutch Reformed Church at Ficksburg. **444** The Dutch Reformed Church at Kroonstad, an important centre for the nearby Free State goldfields. **445** Ficksburg, with its mountainous countryside and healthy, cool climate, has much to offer the tourist in

445

446

447

search of relaxation. **446** Playing bowls at Ficksburg. **447** Horses grazing in a lush region of the eastern Free State – a major horse-breeding area. Horses are not indigenous to South Africa. The first were imported from Java by the Dutch East India Company in 1652, the year that van Riebeeck arrived at the Cape.

448

449

450

448 Angora goats were first imported into South Africa in 1838. Since then an important industry has developed and only the USA and Turkey produce more mohair than South Africa. **449** A fairly common sight on country roads. **450** South Africa's grain yield is greatly affected by the unpredictable weather. **451** View from above Witsieshoek.

452

453

454

455

452 Ownership of the lush fertile valley of the Caledon River which flows past Ficksburg and Maseru was bitterly contested by the Basuto and Freestaters. **453** The fruit of the *Olinia emarginata,* a small but handsome evergreen tree which occurs in sheltered ravines along the foothills of the Drakensberg. It bears these striking fruits in autumn and early winter.
454 Drakensberg foothills in the Qwaqwa Homeland. For the one million South Sotho living outside Lesotho, this Homeland has been established at Witsieshoek. **455** Nelson's Kop near the town of Harrismith.

456

457

458

459

460

456 Young girls carrying fodder. The collecting of fuel and fodder is a major activity in village life. **457** Young Catholic girls attending their first Communion. **458** Woman carrying material for making carpets and brooms.
459 Many Basuto are adept at weaving, a craft introduced by missionaries. Their carpets and tapestries have won international acclaim. **460** Woman carrying melons in the traditional way.

Transvaal

This province boasts a multitude of attractions – amongst them the cosmopolitan city of Johannesburg, the sedate capital Pretoria and, in the Eastern Transvaal, some of South Africa's most spectacular scenery which includes the famous Game Reserve, the Kruger National Park.

The Transvaal's mineral wealth makes it one of the richest areas in the world. More than 50 metals and minerals, including uranium, gold and platinum, are mined here. And, because of the rapid economic growth, it is possible that more than half South Africa's people will live here in the future.

461

461 Johannesburg was established in 1886 after gold had been found on surrounding farms. It was probably named after Johann Rissik and Christiaan Johannes Joubert, who recommended that the area be declared a public goldfield. The Transvaal Government owned the uninhabited farm Randjeslaagte and therefore chose it as the site for the new town. In this way the Government could increase its revenue by the sale of plots or 'stands'. The surveyor, J. E. de Villiers, ignored the contours of the ground and adopted a gridiron plan with all streets running north-south or east-west. No commonages were provided as with other towns because the Government believed that the gold would soon peter out and the miners would go elsewhere. As many stands as possible were therefore created from the available area.

462

463

464

465

466

462 At 10 a.m. on December 8, 1886 the first auction was held, and the first stand offered for sale was bought for half-a-crown (25 cents). **463** Window cleaner's view. **464-466** The old has rapidly made way for the new.
467 A view of densely-populated Hillbrow from the J.G. Strijdom Tower. The phenomenal growth of Johannesburg is illustrated by the following population figures: 1887:2 000 1899:120 000 1960:1 096 000 1970:1 432 634.

467

468

469

470

471

472   473

468 The J.G. Strijdom Tower (269 m). Johannesburg is the largest city in Southern Africa and the third largest in Africa, after Cairo and Alexandria. **469** Johannesburg, from a helicopter controlling traffic. **470** Sunday morning in Johannesburg. **471** A member of the South African Airways ground staff approaches the town terminal. **472** As corner stands are more valuable, President Kruger instructed that there should be more streets. He marked the present positions of Joubert and Von Brandis streets saying: 'There must be streets here!' Hence the narrowness of these streets today. **473** Pedestrians wait for the robot (traffic light) to change.

474

475

476

477

478 479 480 481

482 483 484

474 Central Johannesburg is rapidly changing in appearance. **475** Flower sellers on a street corner. **476** Most of Johannesburg's Asian population originally came from Natal to trade in the Transvaal. **477** Outside the station hawkers do a roaring trade. **478 479** Most of Johannesburg's Blacks are westernized to varying degrees, but from time to time one is struck by the contrast of a Black in tribal dress juxtaposed with a modern tower-block. **480** Vegetable vendor near the city centre. **481** African beadwork for sale. **482** Roof-top pool of a luxury hotel in the city. **483 484** Urban workers hurrying to their jobs.

485

486

487

488

489   490   491

485 City traffic. The Johannesburg City Council's budget is larger than that of the Orange Free State Provincial Administration. More than 2 200 km of streets are cleaned every day and 20 million dustbins emptied annually! **486** Forty-five percent of all cars in Africa are registered in the Republic. **487** Meter maids attempt to solve some of the city's motor congestion problems. **488** A weekend art exhibition. **489** Homeward bound. **490** An aerial view of suburban Johannesburg. **491** Jo'burg attracts young people from all over the country.

492

493

494

495

496

497

492 - 497 Encompassing only a few city blocks, Hillbrow is the most densely-populated area in South Africa. This vibrant, cosmopolitan flatland never sleeps. **498** Flowers bloom in Joubert Park, just below Hillbrow.

499

500

501

499 Sandton City. Huge shopping complexes have been constructed outside the city centre for the convenience of suburban dwellers. 500 Jan Smuts Airport, South Africa's main international airport, boasts modern facilities and a striking terminal. 501 Record bar. 502 A few interesting old shops still exist, like this barber's shop. 503 Neon-lit scene in Hillbrow. 504 Supermarket. 505 Batiks for sale near Sandton. 506 Departmental store. 507 A woman demonstrates weaving at a modern shopping complex in Rosebank. 508 A well-known bookshop in Hillbrow. Many shops in this area remain open late at night.

509

510

511

512

509 510 There were once stock exchanges in Barberton, Kimberley, Cape Town, Pietermaritzburg and Durban, but today only the Johannesburg Stock Exchange remains. It is one of the most important in the world with a total amount of R2 143 million new capital raised in 1973. **511** Traditional beadwork. **512** Pavement café. **513** On the campus of the University of the Witwatersrand, students gather for discussion and debate. This is the largest English-medium university in South Africa with 10 299 students registered in 1974. **514** The new Rand Afrikaans University was established in 1966. In 1975 it had 2 600 students. **515** The Medical Research Centre at the University of the Witwatersrand.

513

514

515

516

516 Anxiety and delight mirrored in the expressions of a huge crowd as they watch Kaiser Chiefs and Bantu Colliers play soccer in Soweto. **517** Soccer is the most popular sport among Blacks, many of whom display great natural ability. **518** Fishing at Zoo Lake. **519** Thousands watch a rugby match at Ellis Park. **520** Motor cycling draws many enthusiasts. **521** One of many golf courses in and around Johannesburg. **522** Sunday afternoon boating on Zoo Lake.

517

518

519

520

521

522

523

524 525 526

523 Pit-stop at Kyalami, venue of the annual South African Grand Prix.
524 At Kyalami racetrack. **525** As many as 100 000 people are attracted
to the Grand Prix. **526** The racetrack has recently been widened and
improved to conform to international standards. **527** Motor racing fans at
Kyalami. **528** The Vaal River, from which the Transvaal derives its name, is
famous for its yellowfish and barbel. Although the Transvaal has no coast-

line, boating and most forms of water-sport are popular. **529** Cricket at the Wanderers. The first recorded match in South Africa was held in 1808 in Cape Town for a stake of one thousand rix-dollars. **530** The Johannesburg Soaring Centre at Baragwanath is the largest gliding club in South Africa. **531** Sports club at Melrose, a suburb of Johannesburg. **532** Tennis at Ellis Park.

534

535

536   537

533 Soweto, South Africa's largest Black housing complex, is situated in the municipal area of Johannesburg. The name is derived from 'South Western Townships'. In 1970 it consisted of 26 towns with an official population figure of 558 798, but the actual figure is known to be much higher.
534 Most people who live in Soweto commute by train to work in the large industrial complexes of the Witwatersrand. **535 536** Blacks have an innate sense of rhythm and love for music and dancing. **537** Outdoor restaurant at Zoo Lake which also has a popular and elegant night-club.

538

539

538 Mine dumps form an integral part of the Witwatersrand scenery. Gold was discovered here in 1886, reputedly by a prospector who thought his find so unimpressive that he left his claim and disappeared in search of better things. He had, in fact, stumbled on the 'Main Reef' of the Witwatersrand, a vast geological basin of gold-bearing rock. Since then seven goldfields have been exploited in the Witwatersrand basin which has produced about one third of all the gold ever won by mankind. **539** Eroded surface of a mine dump near Johannesburg. As much as one ton of rock must be processed to yield half an ounce of gold. **540** Gold refinery. The ore is brought to the surface where it is crushed, washed and chemically processed. The refined molten gold is poured into 400 ounce bars which are 99,6% pure. **541** Mine dumps. **542** Mine on the East Rand. The Witwatersrand mines are among the deepest in the world and drilling is currently carried out at depths of over 3 500 m. Intense heat from within the earth and the constant dangers of flooding and rockbursts necessitate a rigorous training programme for miners.

540

541

542

177

543

544

545

546

547

548

543 Corrugated-iron miner's house. More than 400 000 men work on the mines. **544** Bullion at the South African Reserve Bank which holds and distributes all gold mined in the Republic. **545** Sub-economic housing in Soweto. **546** Pouring gold. **547** Founded on the prosperity of the gold mines, the development of industry and exploitation of minerals such as coal and iron has centred in the Transvaal. The Iron and Steel Industrial Corporation (ISCOR) produces over 3,5 million ingot tons of steel annually. Although ISCOR operates as an independent enterprise, it is financed largely by the State. **548** Pressing moulds for Kruger Rands.

179

549 The Voortrekker Monument, the most imposing and significant in South Africa, was opened on the Day of the Covenant, December 16, 1949. **550** The J.G. Strijdom Memorial in Pretoria. **551** Army headquarters are located in Pretoria. **552** The Palace of Justice overlooking Church Square. Pretoria was named after the Voortrekker leader Andries Pretorius and was originally called Pretoria-Philadelphia. **553** Mirage jet and crew.

552

553

554

555

556

557

554 Old buildings make way for new in central Pretoria. **555** The Union Buildings in Pretoria were designed by Sir Herbert Baker and constructed in 1910-1913. **556** A helping hand. **557** Waiting for a bus.

558

559

560

561

562

558 Pretoria is the fourth largest city in South Africa and has a population of 561 703 (1970 Census). As the administrative capital, a large percentage of the population is made up of civil servants. **559** One of the many fine examples of contemporary architecture. **560** Government offices: the civil service employs 20% of the Republic's White manpower. **561** Relaxing in Church Square, Pretoria. This large square, originally the market-place, was named after the first small thatched Dutch Reformed Church consecrated here in 1857. **562** People-watching.

185

563 Pretoria is famous for its 60 000 jacaranda trees, originally imported from South America. **564** Sunday dress. Pretoria is noted for its many churches, particularly those of the Afrikaans denominations. **565** *Cosmos bipinnatus:* common cosmos, a native of America, is now naturalised in South Africa, particularly on the Highveld. **566** It is only in recent years that advertisers have realised the enormous consumer potential of the Black market. **567** Smiles.

567

568

569

188

570

571

568 ISCOR, Pretoria. **569** Farm on the Highveld. **570** Colliery at Witbank. Although coal had been discovered in various parts of South Africa, serious coal mining commenced only after the discovery of gold and because of the need for power on the Witwatersrand. Half of the annual output is used to generate electricity. Many power stations are being built above coal seams to which they are linked by semi-automatic mining operations. These convey coal direct from the mine-head to the furnaces. **571** Citrus orchard at Zebediela, the largest single orange orchard in the world.

572

573

574

575

576

572 Barberton. When rich gold-bearing reefs were discovered here in 1874, fortune-seekers flocked to this town. However, the discovery of gold on the Witwatersrand caused an exodus and by 1887 Barberton was virtually a ghost town. **573** Pilgrim's Rest, in the Eastern Transvaal, is the site of the oldest gold mine in South Africa. The mine was closed in 1971 and the town is being preserved as a tourist attraction. Some of the old corrugated iron buildings date back to the days of the original gold rush. **574** Krugersdorp, an important gold mining and industrial centre, was named after President Paul Kruger. **575** Carting firewood. **576** Excuse my dust!

577 The Blyde River, with its striking panoramas of the Eastern Transvaal Lowveld, plunges into one of the most spectacular gorges in Africa. A large tract of land on either side of the canyon has been proclaimed a nature reserve. 578 The Three Rondavels in the Blyde River Canyon dominate a gorge whose sides soar to 600 m in places. 579 View from the Long Tom Pass on the road to Sabie in the Eastern Transvaal. The famous gun, Long Tom, used by the Boers in the sieges of Mafeking, Ladysmith and Kimberley, was finally abandoned here. 580 Attractively-situated hotel in the Eastern Transvaal. 581 The potholes of Bourke's Luck, a curious formation eroded by the confluence of the Blyde and Treur Rivers. In 1884 Andries Potgieter and a few men set out to make contact with the Portuguese at Delagoa Bay. After some time, the remaining group assumed that Potgieter and his party had perished and they moved on, naming the river where they had camped Treur (Sorrowful) River. Upon reaching another river, they were overtaken by Potgieter and named this river Blyde (Joyful) River. 582 Cattle being herded along a national road.

583

584

585

586

587

588

583 Entrance to the Sudwala Caves, with ancient artefacts in the foreground. The Sudwala Caves are concealed in the Mankelekele Mountain, north-east of Nelspruit. They were opened to the public in 1964 and since then many new passages and chambers of eroded rock, stalagmites and stalactites have been discovered. **584** Slate quarry near Sabie. **585** A river overflowing its banks in the Eastern Transvaal which has an average annual rainfall of over 700 mm. **586** River in the Sabie district. **587** Felled trees for the Eastern Transvaal's important timber industry. **588** God's Window in the north-eastern Transvaal gives a glorious view of the Lowveld.
589 Since 1903 efforts have been made to save what was left of the indigenous forest and to establish plantations for the increasing timber requirements of the mines.

589

590

591

592

593

594

595

596

597

590 Lisbon Falls, near the Blyde River Canyon, one of many beautiful waterfalls which grace the Eastern Transvaal. **591** Harvesting mealie (maize) stalks for fodder. **592** *Acacia xanthphloea,* the fever tree of the Lowveld. **593** Sheep grazing near Lydenburg. **594** Mountainous scenery near Barberton. **595** The Mac-Mac Falls, near Sabie, tumble 91 m into a deep gorge. The river just above the waterfall was the scene of an alluvial gold rush in 1873. **596 597** Two ways of marketing handwoven baskets.

598 Potatoes are one of South Africa's most important food crops.
599 Harvesting tea. Not even an annual crop of 15 million kg can satisfy this country's needs where the average person consumes 510 cups of tea a year. **600 601** Curing and harvesting tobacco which was probably introduced to South Africa by early Portuguese explorers. The Transvaal is the largest producer in South Africa and approximately one third of the crop is exported. **602** Stable in a remote area of the Northern Transvaal. **603** The Tsonga people are mostly subsistence farmers and cattle owners; the women often remain on the land while the men seek work in towns.
604 Lilac-breasted roller *(Coracias caudata).* **605** The north-western region of the Transvaal has less than 400 mm of rain each year. **606** A lonely Ndebele village. The Ndebele are famous for the brightly-painted walls of their homes. **607** Typical Northern Transvaal scenery, dominated here by the *Aloe marlothii.*

198

608

609

610

608 Farmhands. Agriculture in the Republic relies heavily on unskilled labour. **609** After-school netball practice. Until 1955 the education of Blacks was undertaken by missionary societies and the provincial administrations. Since then the State has assumed responsibility. **610** *Eucomis* and tree ferns *(Cyathea dregei),* on the Wolkberg Mountains, Northern

611

612

613

Transvaal. **611** A gang of workers repairs part of the 19 149 km of railway track in the Republic. The South African Railways employs nearly a quarter of a million people. **612** Young girl in the Northern Transvaal. **613** Ndebele girl near Pretoria. The term Ndebele covers a wide range of people of Nguni origin, spread over parts of the Transvaal and Rhodesia.

614 Baboon *(Papio ursinus)* in the Kruger National Park. This enormous game sanctuary was proclaimed in 1926 and covers an area of more than 20 720 km². It is dotted with picturesque rest camps. Varied wild life and scenery ensure that a visit to the park will be a memorable and exciting experience. **615** Giraffe *(Giraffa camelopardalis).* The Afrikaans word 'kameelperd' is derived from the name 'camelopard'. The giraffe's long neck, which makes it the tallest animal in the world, contains only seven vertibrae and allows for tree-top browsing. **616** Crowned plover *(Stephanibyx coronatus).* **617** The white rhinoceros *(Ceratotherium simum),* with its combination of poor eyesight and low intelligence, is considered by many to be unpredictably dangerous. **618** *Protea transvaalensis.* **619** Crowned guineafowl *(Numida meleagris).* Although once the most

202

621

popular gamebird in Southern Africa, they are now protected.
620 *Androcymbium striatum.* **621** Buffalo *(Syncerus caffer)* are usually found in large herds near water where they often wallow in the mud. Although they spend much of the day resting, buffalo are quick to charge when antagonised and can be one of the most dangerous animals in Africa, often doubling back in their tracks to lie in wait for hapless pursuers.

622 Cheetah *(Acinonyx jubatus)*. **623** The gemsboks' *(Oryx gazella)* handsome horns, when seen in profile, gave rise to the belief that it was the mythical unicorn. **624** Baboon *(Papio ursinus)*. **625** Lion *(Panthera leo)*. The king of the beasts fears no rival and may often be seen basking during the daytime without making any effort to conceal itself. **626** Elephant *(Loxodonta africana)* with unsymmetrical tusks. Tusks are used not only as weapons or to intimidate rivals and enemies, but also as tools for digging. **627** Hippopotami *(Hippopotamus amphibius)*. There are few animals which can match the hippo for sheer strength and the adult has no real enemy apart from man. **628** Serval cat *(Felis serval)*. Its mastery of the two traditional feline hunting techniques – ambush and stalking – allows the serval a wide range of prey. **629** Burchell's zebra *(Equus burchelli)*, one of two remaining species in South Africa. **630** Young male kudu *(Tragelaphus strepsiceros)*. The magnificent spiral horns of the mature male may reach over 1,5 m in length. **631** Springbok *(Antidorcas marsupialis)*. Large numbers of these antelope once inhabited the great plains of South Africa

and are still abundant in the Kalahari. **632** The secretary-bird *(Sagattarius serpentarius),* usually seen striding over the veld with great dignity and deliberation, kills snakes with violent blows from its feet while holding out its wings as a shield. **633** Cape glossy starling *(Lamprocolius nitens phoe-nicopterus).* **634** Crimson-breasted shrike *(Laniarius atro-coccineus).* **635** Because of its speed, agility and grace, the springbok is the national sporting emblem. **636** Elephants and an African sunset – a spectacular way to end the day.

Republic of South Africa

Copyright by Rand McNally & Company, R.L.75.1-5

Meters	Feet
6000	19685
4000	13124
3000	9843
2000	6562
1000	3281
500	1640
200	656
0	0

Kilometers

Statute Miles

Scale 1:6,000,000

One centimeter represents 60 kilometers.
One inch represents approximately 95 miles.

207

List of sources

Africana Museum, Johannesburg	3	17	19	24															
Argus, The, Cape Town	49	71	73	90	121	160	553												
Baker, D	98	101																	
Bird & Leeney	300	328	336	369	379	388	413												
Campey, F	108	299	305	337	350	361													
Cape Archives, Cape Town	1	2	4	6	7	8	10	11	12	13	14	15	20	22	26	27	28	31	
Cape Times, The, Cape Town	34	35	36	37	39	40													
Chamber of Mines, Johannesburg	542																		
Cleaver, D	315	316	349	363	408														
Cubitt, G	43	44	47	52	53	57	61	69	75	77	78	80	82	84	92	94	97	102	
	104	105	116	119	123	125	126	129	131	133	137	138	139	140	141	143	145	146	
	148	151	158	159	162	172	174	176	177	178	184	187	189	190	193	204	205	206	
	208	211	222	224	225	228	229	232	235	236	245	259	262	265	266	270	271	277	
	278	279	281	285	287	294	295	296	304	312	318	319	320	327	329	330	333	348	
	357	359	371	373	374	375	376	377	380	381	382	383	386	389	390	391	392	395	
	403	409	412	420	424	425	426	427	429	430	432	435	440	441	442	447	449	451	
	454	461	467	490	516	517	525	526	527	530	533	534	539	541	545	549	550	559	
	564	565	566	572	578	580	581	582	588	592	594	596	599	600	601	603	604	607	
	610	613	614	615	616	617	618	619	620	621	623	624	625	626	627	628	629	630	
Department of Information, Pretoria	29	30	32	33	38														
Department of Forestry, Pretoria	276	589																	
Du Plessis, J	86																		
Durban Publicity Association	313	343	422																
Fagan, G	182																		
Goldblatt, D	239	256																	
Hughes, L	59	134	244	246	247	269	273	344	366	434	444	455	462	463	465	468	469	470	
	471	474	479	486	487	488	498	513	514	515	518	519	520	521	523	524	528	529	
	531	532	538	540	543	555	587	598	602	605	612								
Iscor, Pretoria	547																		
Jansen, C	87	89	91	93	106	109	118	120	130	142	144	147	149	150	153	154	155	156	
	163	164	165	180	181	183	188	213	214	215	219	220	221	223	226	227	230	231	
	233	234	237	238	241	242	243	248	249	250	251	252	253	254	255	257	258	260	
	264	267	268	272	280	356	398	399	417	418	436	437	551	552	554	568	573	576	
	597																		
John, P	51	54	55	56	58	60	62	63	64	65	66	67	68	74	79	81	83	88	
	107	111	124	197	301	302	303	306	307	308	309	310	311	314	317	321	322	323	
	324	325	326	334	335	338	339	340	341	342	346	347	351	352	353	355	358	360	
	362	364	365	368	370	372	405	406	407	410	411	414	415	464	466	472	473	475	
	476	477	478	480	481	483	484	485	489	491	492	493	494	495	496	497	499	500	
	501	502	503	504	505	506	507	508	509	510	511	512	522	535	536	537	544	546	
	548	556	557	558	560	561	562	567	569	570	571	574	575	583	584	585	586	590	
	591	606	608	609	611														
Jordaan, W	45	70	95	99	100	103	113	115	127	132	152	161	166	171	173	175	179	185	
	186	191	192	209	210	212	216	217	218	595									
Liepner, N	345	367	384																
Malherbe, Dr P. H	112	114	194	195	196	198	200	203											
Mendelssohn Collection, Cape Town	5	16	18	21	23	25													
Mertens, A	170	282	283	284	286	288	289	290	291	292	293	297	298	378	385	387	393	394	
	396	397	400	401	402	404	419												
Morris, J	331	332	416	421	423	438	439	450	482	563	577	579	593						
National Botanical Gardens, Kirstenbosch, Cape Town	453																		
Pratt, A	431																		
Richards, C	622	631	632	633	634	635	636												
Rijksmuseum, Amsterdam	9																		
Rourke, Dr J	135	199	201	202															
Schwager, D	46	48	72	76	85	167	168	169	207	240	261	263	354	428	433	443	445	446	
	448	452	456	457	458	459	460												
South African Library, Cape Town	41																		
Wege, R	42	50	96	110	117	122	128	136	157	274	275								